A Field Guide to the Birds of Bermuda

André Raine

MACMILLAN
CARIBBEAN

Macmillan Education
Between Towns Road, Oxford OX4 3PP
A division of Macmillan Publishers Limited
Companies and representatives throughout the world

www.macmillan-caribbean.com

ISBN 0 333 97106 X

Text © André Raine 2003
Design and illustration © Macmillan Publishers Limited 2003
Photographs © Richard Ground 2003

First published 2003

Typeset by CjB Editorial Plus
Illustrated by Tessa Eccles
Cover design by Gary Fielder, AC Design
Cover photograph by Richard Ground

Printed and bound in Malaysia

2007 2006 2005 2004 2003
10 9 8 7 6 5 4 3 2 1

Contents

To
My father, for inspiration
My mother, for support
and
My brother, for encouragement

Preface

This book aims to give the reader a general overview of Bermuda's avifauna in an easy to read and understandable format. Although there are only 22 resident breeding bird species (and three of these, being sea-birds, are not resident year-round) the complex array of migrants and vagrants that visit the island every year have resulted in a list of approximately 360 different species. As it would not be feasible to include full descriptions for all these species, and indeed some of the more wayward vagrants are unlikely ever to be seen on the island again, only 132 of the more common or distinctive species have been treated with full species accounts. This includes all 22 of the resident species. A full checklist of species recorded in Bermuda, as well as their status and relative abundance, has been provided in Chapter 1.

Chapters 2 and 3 provide a brief introduction to the island and its composite habitats, along with attendant bird species. A general overview of the birds of Bermuda is given in Chapter 4, with discussions on endemics, residents (both natives and introductions), migrants and vagrants, extinctions and conservation issues. Chapter 5 gives reference sources while Chapter 6 discusses the topic of birdwatching itself, with reference to bird anatomy, tips and hints to aid in the 'science' of birdwatching, and appropriate considerations for procuring binoculars. This chapter should hopefully make the reader's birding experience as fulfilling as possible.

The bulk of the book (Chapter 7) is taken up by full species descriptions for the more common species found in Bermuda. This entails a full description of the bird, with key pointers for identification and sexual differences, followed by common habitats where one is likely to find the species. Distinguishing marks of similar species are described followed by species status and relative abundance in Bermuda.

Most birds are illustrated with a full colour photograph for easy reference and comparison. Where possible the photograph used shows the main defining features and distinguishing characteristics that aid in identification.

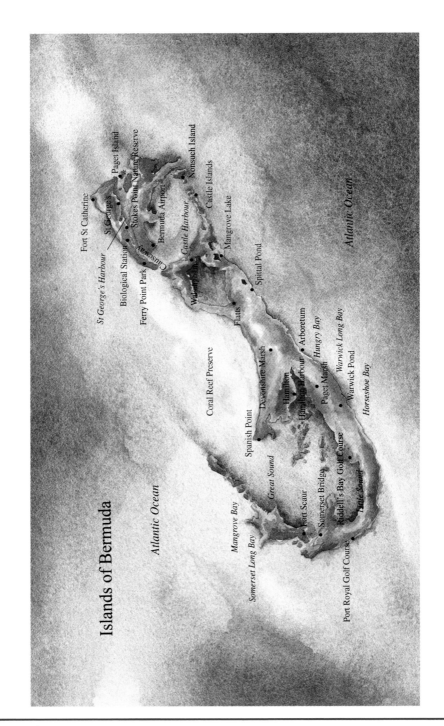

Islands of Bermuda

1 The Birds of Bermuda: A Checklist

On the following pages is a checklist of all birds currently recorded as having visited the islands of Bermuda. The common name and scientific name are followed by designations and abundance ratings to allow the reader to ascertain how likely he or she is to actually find the bird in Bermuda.

Designation

The species is given a designation that entails what its relationship is with the island. This consists of the following categories:

R, **Resident** – a species that breeds in Bermuda and arrived on the island naturally.

R(e), **Endemic** – a species (or sub-species) that is found only in Bermuda.

R(s), **Seasonal breeder** – a species that is resident in Bermuda during the breeding season, but which is absent at other times.

R(i), **Introduced** – a species that breeds in Bermuda, but which was introduced to the island by humans.

M, **Migrant** – a species that stops over in Bermuda on its way to, or from, its seasonal breeding grounds.

P, **Pelagic migrant** – a species that passes by far offshore on its way to, or from, its seasonal breeding grounds. Individuals may also be found on occasion in harbours and inland water bodies during these migration periods.

V, **Vagrant** – a species for which Bermuda is not on its usual migration route and which is often far from its original destination.

FB, **Former breeder** – a species that used to breed in Bermuda but has unfortunately since ceased to breed on the islands. Note that although it may no longer breed in Bermuda, it may still be found as a migrant or vagrant.

NB, **New breeding record** – a species that has only recently started breeding on Bermuda.

Abundance

Following the previous category of designation, each species is given a rating for its relative abundance in Bermuda. It is important to remember that this rating is only for the relevant time of year. If a species is listed as either a 'Seasonal breeder' or 'Migrant', then its abundance will only be valid for the time of year when the species is commonly found in Bermuda. For example, the White-tailed Tropicbird (*Phaethon lepturus*) is 'Common' only during the breeding season and at other times of the year it is not present. Similarly the American Redstart (*Steophaga ruticilla*) is 'Common' only during migration; at other times it should be considered 'Uncommon' as most individuals leave the island and continue to their wintering grounds in South America, and only a few remain behind as winter residents. Abundance ratings fall into the following categories:

A, Abundant – a species that is present on the island in large numbers and will be encountered every time its habitat is searched.

C, Common – a species that is present on the island in good numbers and should be seen every time its habitat is entered.

F, Frequent – a species that is relatively common on the island and one that should be seen if its habitat is searched carefully enough.

U, Uncommon – a species that appears infrequently on the island and one that is unlikely to be seen every time its habitat is searched.

O, Occasional – a species that appears on the island erratically and infrequently over the years, and one that is unlikely to be seen in any given year.

R, Rare – the true vagrants. Bewildered individuals that are exceptionally off course and that have only been recorded on a handful of occasions over the years.

Special note: If a rating of 'Rare' is given to a resident species, then it means that only few individuals remain and it is very unlikely that they will be seen in Bermuda.

Birds of Bermuda*

Common Name	Latin Name	Designation	Abundance
Gaviidae (Loons)			
1. Common Loon	*Gavia immer*	V	R
2. Pacific Loon	*Gavia pacifica*	V	R
Podicipedidae (Grebes)			
3. Red-necked Grebe	*Podiceps grisegena*	V	R
4. Horned Grebe	*Podiceps auritus*	V	U
5. Eared Grebe	*Podiceps nigricollis*	V	R
6. **Pied-billed Grebe**	*Podilymbus podiceps*	M/NB	C
Procellariidae (Shearwaters and Petrels)			
7. Cory's Shearwater	*Calonectris diomedea*	P	F
8. **Greater Shearwater**	*Puffinus gravis*	P	A
9. Sooty Shearwater	*Puffinus griseus*	P	F
10. **Manx Shearwater**	*Puffinus puffinus*	P	C
11. Audubon's Shearwater	*Puffinus lherminieri*	P/FB	R
12. **Cahow**	*Pterodroma cahow*	R(e)(s)	R
13. Black-capped Petrel	*Pterodroma hasitata*	V	R
Hydrobatidae (Storm Petrels)			
14. Leach's Storm-Petrel	*Oceanodroma leucorhoa*	P	F
15. Wilson's Storm-Petrel	*Oceanites oceanicus*	P	F
Fregatidae (Frigatebirds)			
16. Magnificent Frigatebird	*Fregata magnificens*	V	R
Phaethontidae (Tropicbirds)			
17. Red-billed Tropicbird	*Phaethon aethereus*	V	R
18. **White-tailed Tropicbird**	*Phaethon lepturus*	R(s)	A
Pelecanidae (Pelicans)			
19. Brown Pelican	*Pelecanus occidentalis*	V	U
Sulidae (Boobies and Gannets)			
20. Brown Booby	*Sula leucogaster*	V	U
21. Masked Booby	*Sula dactylatra*	V	R
22. Northern Gannet	*Morus bassanus*	V	R
Phalacrocoracidae (Cormorants)			
23. Great Cormorant	*Phalacrocorax carbo*	V	F
24. **Double-crested Cormorant**	*Phalacrocorax auritus*	V	C
Ardeidae (Herons and Bitterns)			
25. **Great Blue Heron**	*Ardea herodias*	M	C

* The birds whose common names are in **bold** type in this table are described in full in the species listing in Chapter 7.

Common Name	Latin Name	Designation	Abundance
26. **Green Heron**	*Butorides striatus*	V/NB	C
27. **Little Blue Heron**	*Egretta caerulea*	V	F
28. **Tricolored Heron**	*Egretta tricolor*	V	F
29. **Snowy Egret**	*Egretta thula*	V	F
30. Little Egret	*Egretta garzetta*	V	R
31. **Cattle Egret**	*Bubulcus ibis*	V	C
32. **Great Egret**	*Casmerodius albus*	V	F
33. Black-crowned Night Heron	*Nycticorax nycticorax*	V	O
34. **Yellow-crowned Night Heron**	*Nyctanassa violacea*	R(i)	C
35. Least Bittern	*Ixobrychus exilis*	V	U
36. **American Bittern**	*Botaurus lentiginosus*	V	U

Threskiornithidae (Ibises and Spoonbills)

37. **Glossy Ibis**	*Plegadis falcinellus*	V	U
38. White Ibis	*Eudocimus albus*	V	O

Gruidae (Cranes)

39. Sandhill Crane	*Grus Canadensis*	V	R

Phoenicopteridae (Flamingos)

40. Greater Flamingo	*Phoenicopterus ruber*	V/escapee	R

Anatidae (Swans, Geese and Ducks)

41. Mute Swan	*Cygnus olor*	V	R
42. Tundra Swan	*Cygnus columbianus*	V	R
43. **Canada Goose**	*Branta canadensis*	V	F
44. Brant Goose	*Branta bernicla*	V	R
45. **Snow Goose**	*Chen caerulescens*	V	F
46. Greater White-fronted Goose	*Anser albifrons*	V	R
47. Fulvous Whistling-Duck	*Dendrocygna bicolor*	V	F
48. West Indian Whistling-Duck	*Dendrocygna arborea*	V	R
49. **Mallard**	*Anas platyrhynchos*	R(i)/V	C
50. **American Black Duck**	*Anas rubripes*	V	F
51. Gadwall	*Anas strepera*	V	R
52. Northern Pintail	*Anas acuta*	V	U
53. **Green-winged Teal**	*Anas crecca*	V	F
54. **Blue-winged Teal**	*Anas discors*	M	C
55. Garganey	*Anas querquedula*	V	R
56. Eurasian Wigeon	*Anas penelope*	V	R
57. **American Wigeon**	*Anas americana*	V	U
58. Northern Shoveler	*Anas clypeata*	V	U
59. Wood Duck	*Aix sponsa*	V	O
60. Ferruginous Duck	*Aythya nyroca*	V	R
61. Redhead	*Aythya americana*	V	U

Common Name	Latin Name	Designation	Abundance
62. **Ring-necked Duck**	*Aythya collaris*	V	F
63. Tufted Duck	*Aythya fuligula*	V	U
64. **Canvasback**	*Aythya valisineria*	V	U
65. Greater Scaup	*Aythya marila*	V	O
66. **Lesser Scaup**	*Aythya affinis*	V	U
67. **Common Goldeneye**	*Bucephala clangula*	V	U
68. **Bufflehead**	*Bucephala albeola*	V	O
69. Long-tailed Duck	*Clangula hyemalis*	V	R
70. White-winged Scoter	*Melanitta fusca*	V	R
71. Surf Scoter	*Melanitta perspicillata*	V	U
72. Black Scoter	*Melanitta nigra*	V	U
73. Ruddy Duck	*Oxyura jamaicensis*	V	O
74. **Hooded Merganser**	*Lophodytes cucullatus*	V	O
75. Common Merganser	*Mergus merganser*	V	O
76. **Red-breasted Merganser**	*Mergus serrator*	V	U

Rallidae (Rails, Gallinules and Coots)

Common Name	Latin Name	Designation	Abundance
77. Clapper Rail	*Rallus longirostrus*	V	R
78. Virginia Rail	*Rallus limicola*	V	O
79. **Sora Rail**	*Porzana carolina*	V	F
80. Yellow Rail	*Coturnicops noveboracensis*	V	R
81. Black Rail	*Laterallus jamaicensis*	V	R
82. Corn Crake	*Crex crex*	V	R
83. Purple Gallinule	*Porphyrula martinica*	V	O
84. **Common Gallinule (Moorhen)**	*Gallinula chloropus*	R/M	C
85. **American Coot**	*Fulica americana*	R/M	A

Recurvirostridae (Avocets and Stilts)

Common Name	Latin Name	Designation	Abundance
86. Black-necked Stilt	*Himantopus mexicanus*	V	U
87. American Avocet	*Recurvirostra americana*	V	O

Charadriidae (Plovers and Turnstones)

Common Name	Latin Name	Designation	Abundance
88. Northern Lapwing	*Vanellus vanellus*	V	R
89. **Semipalmated Plover**	*Charadrius semipalmatus*	M	C
90. Piping Plover	*Charadrius melodus*	V	U
91. Wilson's Plover	*Charadrius wilsonia*	V	R
92. **Killdeer**	*Charadrius vociferus*	M	C
93. Eurasian Dotterel	*Charadrius morinellus*	V	R
94. **American Lesser Golden Plover**	*Pluvialis dominica*	M	F

Common Name	Latin Name	Designation	Abundance
95. Pacific Golden Plover	*Pluvialis fulva*	V	R
96. **Black-bellied Plover**	*Pluvialis squatarola*	M	C

Scolopacidae (Sandpipers, Woodcock, Snipe and Phalaropes)

Common Name	Latin Name	Designation	Abundance
97. American Woodcock	*Scolopax minor*	V	U
98. **Common (Wilson's) Snipe**	*Gallinago gallinago*	M	C
99. Eurasian Curlew	*Numenius arquata*	V	R
100. **Whimbrel**	*Numenius phaeopus*	V	U
101. Upland Sandpiper	*Bartramia longicauda*	M	O
102. **Spotted Sandpiper**	*Actitis macularia*	M	C
103. **Solitary Sandpiper**	*Tringa solitaria*	M	C
104. Wood Sandpiper	*Tringa glareola*	V	R
105. Common Greenshank	*Tringa nebularia*	V	R
106. **Greater Yellowlegs**	*Tringa melanoleuca*	M	F
107. **Lesser Yellowlegs**	*Tringa flavipes*	M	C
108. Willet	*Catoptrophorus semipalmatus*	V	O
109. **Ruddy Turnstone**	*Arenaria interpres*	M	A
110. Red Knot	*Calidris canutus*	M	O
111. Red-necked Stint	*Calidris ruficollis*	V	R
112. Little Stint	*Calidris minuta*	V	R
113. **Pectoral Sandpiper**	*Calidris melanotos*	M	C
114. White-rumped Sandpiper	*Calidris fuscicollis*	M	O
115. Baird's Sandpiper	*Calidris bairdii*	V	U
116. **Least Sandpiper**	*Calidris minutilla*	M	C
117. Sharp-tailed Sandpiper	*Calidris acuminata*	V	R
118. Curlew Sandpiper	*Calidris ferruginea*	V	R
119. Dunlin	*Calidris alpina*	V	O
120. **Stilt Sandpiper**	*Calidris himantopus*	M	F
121. **Semipalmated Sandpiper**	*Calidris pusilla*	M	A
122. Western Sandpiper	*Calidris mauri*	V	F
123. **Sanderling**	*Calidris alba*	M	C
124. **Short-billed Dowitcher**	*Limnodromus griseus*	V	U
125. Long-billed Dowitcher	*Limnodromus scolopaceus*	V	O
126. Buff-breasted Sandpiper	*Tryngites subrufricollis*	V	O
127. Hudsonian Godwit	*Limosa haemastica*	V	U
128. Bar-tailed Godwit	*Limosa lapponica*	V	R
129. Ruff	*Philomachus pugnax*	V	O
130. Red Phalarope	*Phalaropus fulicaria*	P	F
131. Red-necked Phalarope	*Phalaropus lobatus*	P	F
132. **Wilson's Phalarope**	*Phalaropus tricolor*	V	O

Laridae (Jaegers, Skuas, Gulls and Terns)

Common Name	Latin Name	Designation	Abundance
133. **Great Skua**	*Catharacta skua*	P	F

Common Name	Latin Name	Designation	Abundance
134. South Polar Skua	*Catharacta maccormicki*	P	F
135. **Pomarine Jaeger**	*Stercorarius pomarinus*	P	F
136. **Parasitic Jaeger**	*Stercorarius parasiticus*	P	F
137. Long-tailed Jaeger	*Stercorarius longicaudus*	P	F
138. Glaucous Gull	*Larus hyperboreus*	V	R
139. Iceland Gull	*Larus glaucoides*	V	R
140. **Great Black-backed Gull**	*Larus marinus*	V	F
141. **Lesser Black-backed Gull**	*Larus fuscus*	V	O
142. **Herring Gull**	*Larus argentatus*	V	F
143. **Ring-billed Gull**	*Larus delawarensis*	V	C
144. Black-headed Gull	*Larus ridibundus*	V	O
145. Franklin's Gull	*Larus pipixcan*	V	R
146. Laughing Gull	*Larus atricilla*	V	O
147. **Bonaparte's Gull**	*Larus philadelphia*	V	O
148. Little Gull	*Larus minutus*	V	R
149. **Black-legged Kittiwake**	*Rissa tridactyla*	V	F
150. Sabine's Gull	*Xema sabini*	V	R
151. **Gull-billed Tern**	*Sterna nilotica*	V	U
152. Forster's Tern	*Sterna forsteri*	V	O
153. **Common Tern**	*Sterna hirundo*	M/R(s)	C
154. **Arctic Tern**	*Sterna paradisaea*	P	C
155. Roseate Tern	*Sterna dougallii*	V	U
156. **Sooty Tern**	*Sterna fuscata*	V/FB	U
157. **Least Tern**	*Sterna antillarum*	V	U
158. Bridled Tern	*Sterna anaethetus*	V	R
159. Royal Tern	*Sterna maxima*	V	O
160. Sandwich Tern	*Sterna sandvicensis*	V	U
161. Caspian Tern	*Sterna caspia*	V	R
162. Large-billed Tern	*Phaetusa simplex*	V	R
163. **Black Tern**	*Chilidonias niger*	V	O
164. Brown Noddy	*Anous stolidus*	V	R
165. White Tern	*Gygis alba*	V	R
166. Black Skimmer	*Rynchops niger*	V	O
Alcidae (Auks and Puffins)			
167. Dovekie	*Alle alle*	V	R
168. Atlantic Puffin	*Fratercula arctica*	V	R
Pandionidae (Ospreys)			
169. **Osprey**	*Pandion haliaetus*	M	F
Cathartidae (American Vultures)			
170. Turkey Vulture	*Cathartes aura*	V	R

Common Name	Latin Name	Designation	Abundance
Accipitridae (Hawks and Eagles)			
171. **Swallow-tailed Kite**	*Elanoides forficatus*	V	O
172. Northern Goshawk	*Accipiter gentilis*	V	O
173. **Sharp-shinned Hawk**	*Accipiter striatus*	V	O
174. Cooper's Hawk	*Accipiter cooperii*	V	R
175. Red-tailed Hawk	*Buteo jamaicensis*	V	R
176. Rough-legged Hawk	*Buteo lagopus*	V	R
177. Bald Eagle	*Haliaeetus leucocephalus*	V	R
178. Booted Eagle	*Hieraaetus pennatus*	V	R
179. Northern Harrier	*Circus cyaneus*	V	R
Falconidae (Falcons)			
180. **Peregrine Falcon**	*Falco peregrinus*	M	O
181. Gry Falcon	*Falco rusticolus*	V	R
182. **Merlin**	*Falco columbarius*	V	C
183. Eurasian Kestrel	*Falco tinnunculus*	V	R
184. **American Kestrel**	*Falco sparverius*	V	F
Columbidae (Doves and Pigeons)			
185. **Rock Dove (Feral Pigeon)**	*Columba livia*	R(i)	A
186. **Mourning Dove**	*Zenaida macroura*	R/M	A
187. **Common Ground-Dove**	*Columbina passerina*	R	C
Cuculidae (Cuckoos)			
188. **Yellow-billed Cuckoo**	*Coccyzus americanus*	V	F
189. Black-billed Cuckoo	*Coccyzus erythropthalmus*	V	O
Tytonidae (Barn Owls)			
190. **Barn Owl**	*Tyto alba*	R	F
Strigidae (Typical Owls)			
191. Long-eared Owl	*Asio otus*	V	R
192. **Short-eared Owl**	*Asio flammeus*	V	O
193. Great-horned Owl	*Bubo virginianus*	V	R
194. Barred Owl	*Strix varia*	V	R
195. Snowy Owl	*Nyctea scandiaca*	V	R
196. Eastern Screech Owl	*Otus asio*	V	R
197. **Northern Saw-whet Owl**	*Aegolius acadicus*	V	U
198. Northern Hawk Owl	*Surnia ulula*	V	R
Caprimulgidae (Nightjars)			
199. Whip-poor-will	*Caprimulgus vociferus*	V	R
200. **Common Nighthawk**	*Chordeiles minor*	V	F
201. Lesser Nighthawk	*Chordeiles acutipennis*	V	R

Common Name	Latin Name	Designation	Abundance
Apodidae (Swifts)			
202. **Chimney Swift**	*Chaetura pelagica*	V	O
203. Black Swift	*Cypseloides niger*	V	R
204. Common Swift	*Apus apus*	V	R
Trochilidae (Hummingbirds)			
205. **Ruby-throated Hummingbird**	*Archilochus colubris*	V	U
Alcedinidae (Kingfishers)			
206. **Belted Kingfisher**	*Ceryle alcyon*	M	F
Picidae (Woodpeckers)			
207. Northern Flicker	*Colaptes auratus*	V	R
208. Red-headed Woodpecker	*Melanerpes erythrocephalus*	V	R
209. **Yellow-bellied Sapsucker**	*Sphyrapicus varius*	V	O
210. **Downy Woodpecker**	*Picoides pubescens*	V	U
Tyrannidae (Tyrant Flycatchers)			
211. **Eastern Kingbird**	*Tyrannus tyrannus*	V	O
212. Gray Kingbird	*Tyrannus dominicensis*	V	R
213. Western Kingbird	*Tyrannus verticalis*	V	U
214. Tropical Kingbird	*Tyrannus melancholicus*	V	R
215. Fork-tailed Flycatcher	*Tyrannus savana*	V	R
216. **Greater Kiskadee**	*Pitangus sulphuratus*	R(i)	A
217. **Great Crested Flycatcher**	*Myiarchus crinitus*	V	O
218. Ash-throated Flycatcher	*Myiarchus cinerascens*	V	R
219. **Eastern Wood-Pewee**	*Contopus virens*	V	O
220. Olive-sided Flycatcher	*Contopus borealis*	V	U
221. Eastern Phoebe	*Sayornis phoebe*	V	O
222. Say's Phoebe	*Sayornis saya*	V	R
223. Yellow-bellied Flycatcher	*Empidonax flaviventris*	V	U
224. Acadian Flycatcher	*Empidonax virescens*	V	R
225. **Willow Flycatcher**	*Empidonax traillii*	V	U
226. Alder Flycatcher	*Empidonax alnorum*	V	U
227. Least Flycatcher	*Empidonax minimus*	V	U
Alaudidae (Larks)			
228. Eurasian Skylark	*Alauda arvensis*	V	R
229. **Horned Lark**	*Eremophila alpestris*	V	F
Hirundinidae (Swallows and Martins)			
230. **Tree Swallow**	*Tachycineta bicolor*	M	O

Common Name	Latin Name	Designation	Abundance
231. **Purple Martin**	*Progne subis*	M	F
232. Common House Martin	*Delichon urbica*	V	R
233. **Bank Swallow**	*Riparia riparia*	V	O
234. **Barn Swallow**	*Hirundo rustica*	M	C
235. Cave Swallow	*Hirundo fulva*	V	R
236. **Cliff Swallow**	*Hirundo pyrrhonota*	V	O
237. Northern Rough-winged Swallow	*Stelgidopteryx serripennis*	V	U
Corvidae (Crows and Jays)			
238. Blue Jay	*Cyanocitta cristata*	V	R
239. **Common (American) Crow**	*Corvus brachyrhynchos*	R(i)	C
Certhiidae (Creepers)			
240. Brown Creeper	*Certhia americana*	V	U
Sittidae (Nuthatches)			
241. White-breasted Nuthatch	*Sitta carolinensis*	V	R
242. Red-breasted Nuthatch	*Sitta canadensis*	V	U
Troglodytidae (Wrens)			
243. House Wren	*Troglodytes aedon*	V	R
244. Winter Wren	*Troglodytes troglodytes*	V	R
245. Marsh Wren	*Cistothorus palustris*	V	R
Muscicapidae (Thrushes)			
246. Golden-crowned Kinglet	*Regulus satrapa*	V	U
247. Ruby-crowned Kinglet	*Regulus calendula*	V	O
248. **Eastern Bluebird**	*Sialia sialis*	R	F
249. Wood Thrush	*Hylocichla mustelina*	V	O
250. **Hermit Thrush**	*Catharus guttatus*	V	O
251. **Swainson's Thrush**	*Catharus ustulatus*	M	O
252. Gray-cheeked Thrush	*Catharus minimus*	M	O
253. Bicknell's Thrush	*Catharis minimus bicknelli*	V	R
254. Veery	*Catharus fuscescens*	V	O
255. Varied Thrush	*Ixoreus migratorius*	V	R
256. American Robin	*Turdus migratorius*	V	O
257. Northern Wheatear	*Oenanthe oenanthe*	V	O
258. Siberian Flycatcher	*Muscicapa sibirica*	V	R
Laniidae (Shrikes)			
259. Northern Shrike	*Lanius excubitor*	V	U
260. Loggerhead Shrike	*Lanius ludovicianus*	V	R
Mimidae (Mimic Thrushes)			
261. **Grey Catbird**	*Dumetella carolinensis*	R	A

Common Name	Latin Name	Designation	Abundance
262. Northern Mockingbird	*Mimus polyglottos*	V	U
263. Brown Thrasher	*Toxostoma rufum*	V	R
Motacillidae (Pipits and Wagtails)			
264. **American Pipit**	*Anthus rubescens*	V	F
Bombycillidae (Waxwings)			
265. **Cedar Waxwing**	*Bombycilla cedrorum*	V	F
Sturnidae (Starlings)			
266. **Starling**	*Sturnus vulgaris*	R(i)	A
Vireonidae (Vireos)			
267. **Bermuda White-eyed Vireo**	*Vireo griseus bermudiensis*	R(e)	C
268. American White-eyed Vireo	*Vireo griseus griseus*	V	O
269. Yellow-throated Vireo	*Vireo flavifrons*	V	O
270. Blue-Headed Vireo	*Vireo solitarius*	V	O
271. **Black-whiskered Vireo**	*Vireo altiloquus*	V	U
272. **Red-eyed Vireo**	*Vireo olivaceus*	V	C
273. Philadelphia Vireo	*Vireo philadelphicus*	V	O
274. Warbling Vireo	*Vireo gilvus*	V	O
Parulidae (Warblers)			
275. **Prothonotary Warbler**	*Protonotaria citrea*	M	F
276. Golden-winged Warbler	*Vermivora chrysoptera*	V	O
277. Blue-winged Warbler	*Vermivora pinus*	V	O
278. Tennessee Warbler	*Vermivora peregrina*	V	O
279. Orange-crowned Warbler	*Vermivora celata*	V	O
280. Nashville Warbler	*Vermivora ruficapilla*	V	O
281. **Northern Parula**	*Parula americana*	M	F
282. **Black-and-White Warbler**	*Mniotilta varia*	V	C
283. **Magnolia Warbler**	*Dendroica magnolia*	V	F
284. **Cape May Warbler**	*Dendroica tigrina*	V	C
285. **Black-throated Blue Warbler**	*Dendroica caerulescens*	V	U
286. **Yellow-rumped (Myrtle) Warbler**	*Dendroica coronata*	M	C
287. Townsend's Warbler	*Dendroica townsendi*	V	R
288. **Black-throated Green Warbler**	*Dendroica virens*	V	O
289. Cerulean Warbler	*Dendroica cerulea*	V	R
290. Blackburnian Warbler	*Dendroica fusca*	V	O
291. Yellow-throated Warbler	*Dendroica dominica*	V	O
292. Chestnut-sided Warbler	*Dendroica pensylvanica*	V	O

Common Name	Latin Name	Designation	Abundance
293. Bay-breasted Warbler	*Dendroica castanea*	V	O
294. **Blackpoll Warbler**	*Dendroica striata*	M	C
295. Pine Warbler	*Dendroica pinus*	V	O
296. **Yellow Warbler**	*Dendroica petechia*	V	C
297. Prairie Warbler	*Dendroica discolor*	V	O
298. **Palm Warbler**	*Dendroica palmarum*	V	C
299. Kentucky Warbler	*Oporornis formosus*	V	O
300. Connecticut Warbler	*Oporornis agilis*	M	O
301. Mourning Warbler	*Oporornis philadelphia*	V	O
302. Hooded Warbler	*Wilsonia citrina*	V	O
303. Wilson's Warbler	*Wilsonia pusilla*	V	U
304. Canada Warbler	*Wilsonia canadensis*	V	O
305. Swainson's Warbler	*Limnothlypis swainsonii*	V	U
306. Worm-eating Warbler	*Helmitheros vermivorus*	V	O
307. **Ovenbird**	*Seiurus aurocapillus*	M	F
308. **Northern Waterthrush**	*Seiurus noveboracensis*	M	C
309. Louisiana Waterthrush	*Seiurus motacilla*	V	O
310. **Common Yellowthroat**	*Geothlypis trichas*	V	C
311. Yellow-breasted Chat	*Icteria virens*	V	U
312. **American Redstart**	*Setophaga ruticilla*	M	C
Emberezidae (Sparrows, Buntings, Grosbeaks, etc.)			
313. **Northern Cardinal**	*Cardinalis cardinalis*	R(i)	C
314. Rose-breasted Grosbeak	*Pheucticus ludovicianus*	V	O
315. **Blue Grosbeak**	*Guiraca caerulea*	V	F
316. **Indigo Bunting**	*Passerina cyanea*	M	C
317. Painted Bunting	*Passerina ciris*	V	R
318. Dickcissel	*Spiza americana*	V	U
319. Lark Sparrow	*Chondestes grammacus*	V	R
320. Savannah Sparrow	*Passerculus sandwichensis*	V	O
321. Grasshopper Sparrow	*Ammodramus savannarum*	V	O
322. Sharp-tailed Sparrow	*Ammodramus caudacutus*	V	R
323. Vesper Sparrow	*Pooectes gramineus*	V	R
324. **Chipping Sparrow**	*Spizella passerina*	V	O
325. Clay-coloured Sparrow	*Spizella pallida*	V	O
326. Field Sparrow	*Spizella pusilla*	V	R
327. Dark-eyed Junco	*Junco hyemalis*	V	O

Common Name	Latin Name	Designation	Abundance
328. White-crowned Sparrow	*Zonotrichia leucophrys*	V	O
329. White-throated Sparrow	*Zonotrichia albicollis*	V	O
330. Fox Sparrow	*Passerella iliaca*	V	U
331. Lincoln's Sparrow	*Melospiza lincolnii*	V	O
332. Swamp Sparrow	*Melospiza georgiana*	V	U
333. Song Sparrow	*Melospiza melodia*	V	U
334. Lapland Longspur	*Calcarius lapponicus*	V	R
335. **Snow Bunting**	*Plectrophenax nivalis*	V	U

Icteridae (Blackbirds and Orioles)

336. **Bobolink**	*Dolichonyx oryzivorus*	M	C
337. Eastern Meadowlark	*Sturnella magna*	V	R
338. Red-winged Blackbird	*Agelaius phoeniceus*	V	O
339. Yellow-headed Blackbird	*Xanthocephalus xanthocephalus*	V	R
340. Rusty Blackbird	*Euphagus carolinus*	V	R
341. Common Grackle	*Quiscalus quiscula*	V	R
342. Brown-headed Cowbird	*Molothrus ater*	V	R
343. Orchard Oriole	*Icterus spurius*	V	R
344. **Baltimore Oriole**	*Icterus galbula*	V	F

Thraupidae (Tanagers)

345. Scarlet Tanager	*Piranga olivacea*	V	O
346. Summer Tanager	*Piranga rubra*	V	U

Ploceidae (Weaver Finches)

347. **House Sparrow**	*Passer domesticus*	R(i)	A

Fringillidae (Finches)

348. Pine Siskin	*Carduelis pinus*	V	O
349. **European Goldfinch**	*Carduelis carduelis*	R(i)	F
350. American Goldfinch	*Carduelis tristis*	V	R
351. Common Redpoll	*Carduelis flammea*	V	O
352. Red Crossbill	*Loxia curvirostra*	V	R
353. White-winged Crossbill	*Loxia leucoptera*	V	R
354. Pine Grosbeak	*Pinicola enucleator*	V	R
355. Purple Finch	*Carpodacus purpureus*	V	R
356. Evening Grosbeak	*Coccothraustes vespertinus*	V	U

Estrildidae (Waxbills and allies)

357. **Orange-cheeked Waxbill**	*Estrilda melopoda*	R(i)	R
358. **Common Waxbill**	*Estrilda astrild*	R(i)	R

New species recorded in 2002/2003

The American White Pelican (*Pelecanus erythrorhynchos*) was first recorded in Bermuda in December 2002. It is a member of the Pelecanidae (Pelicans) family.
Designation V
Abundance R

The Reddish Egret (*Egretta rufescens*) was recorded for the first time in Bermuda in January 2003. It is a member of the Ardeidae (Herons and Bitterns) family.
Designation V
Abundance R

The Mississippi Kite (*Ictinia mississippiensis*) was recorded for the first time in Bermuda in May 2002. It is a member of the Accipitridae (Hawks and Eagles) family.
Desigation V
Abundance R

Antillean Nighthawk (*Chordeiles gundlachii*) has just (2003) been recorded in Bermuda. It is a member of Caprimulgidae (Nightjar) family.
Desigation V
Abundance R

2 The Islands of Bermuda (by David F. Raine)

Bermuda is a fascinating group of islands in the North Atlantic. Located approximately 1000 miles (1600 km) north of the Bahamas, and 600 miles off the coast of the United States, Bermuda enjoys a sub-tropical climate and a shoreline washed by crystal waters warmed by the Gulf Stream.

Bermuda is unusual in that there were no indigenous people, indeed no permanent human inhabitants, until the start of the seventeenth century. In 1609, there occurred the shipwrecking of the *Sea Venture* which, under Captain Christopher Newport, was on its way from England to the fledgling colony at Jamestown, in Virginia. It was not the first ship – nor indeed the last – to run afoul of the complicated network of coral reefs that encircle Bermuda. It was, however, perhaps the most significant, because the events of that disaster led directly to the colonisation of Bermuda.

Marooned for a period of 10 months, the passengers and crew dedicated their time to building two slightly smaller vessels with which to proceed on their way. While there, they also mapped the area and compiled the definitive listings of Bermuda's flora, fauna and marine life. Thus, when they finally embarked on the completion of their voyage in 1610, they had a vast, unprecedented body of information about Bermuda and a determination to recommend to the Virginia Company in London that Bermuda should be colonised. The first settlers arrived aboard *The Plough* in 1612 and found what Mark Twain would later come to describe as 'Paradise on Earth'. It was certainly idyllic.

The natural vegetation consisted of an extensive forest dominated by cedar trees and palmettos; the rocky coast was draped with low-lying endemic shrubs, and flowering vines crawled along the edges of the pink beaches. Fish were abundant everywhere, their bright hues creating colourful flecks and flashes across the surface of otherwise perfectly clear water. During the daytime, the air was filled with birdlife gliding overhead or swooping among the breaking waves; at night, cahows emerged from the darkness of the ocean to come and feed their young, nestled carefully among island burrows. The unique Bermuda rock lizard, a skink, scurried silently among the shadows, seeking refuge from the relentless sun. Crabs ambled leisurely across the beaches, concerned only with the perpetual probing of hungry herons. Whales patrolled the horizon and the heads of turtles could be seen bobbing up and down close to shore. By the end of the seventeenth century, however, much of this natural landscape had been permanently devastated by human encroachment and hunger.

Today, Bermuda has a population of slightly in excess of 67,000 people, and the inland scenery is dominated by the distinctive pastel shades and white roofs that typify contemporary domestic architecture. Nevertheless, these islands have managed to sustain an intriguing diversity of natural habitats, each supporting unique, carefully protected ecosystems. An active participant in the global Biodiversity Project, several remarkable and specific programmes have been successfully undertaken since the 1940s, including those focusing on endemics such as the cahow and skink. Similarly, under the auspices of the Bermuda Zoological Society, a turtle breeding programme has attained remarkable successes and it is anticipated that hatchlings will eventually return to their native homeland in order to breed, with the same regularity as that of their predecessors.

Probably the most profound undertaking of the twentieth century has been the ongoing effort to restore the natural pre-colonial environment at remote Nonsuch Island. A truly extraordinary project, initiated by Bermuda's pioneering conservationist, David Wingate, has paid meticulous attention to the intricacies of reintroducing those forms of flora and fauna which the first settlers discovered 400 years ago. On the basis of the success of these endeavours, carefully supervised tours to this precarious site have now been made available to the general public.

Through the combined efforts of various government agencies, private organisations and a growing number of sensitive individuals, small but sustainable pockets of Bermuda's natural environment embrace everything from mangrove swamps to beaches, bays and foreshores. Several different forms of forest and woodland have survived, and selected fish breeding grounds have become protected areas, along with the entire coral reef network. One incidental but major benefit of the island's nine golf courses is that such man-made developments offer landscaped ponds and wooded enclaves which attract resident and transient birds on a regular basis! The ongoing enactment of different pieces of legislation helps to ensure that any additional depletion of Bermuda's natural environment will be either halted altogether or significantly diminished.

Today, Bermuda has become an increasingly important location for serious scientific researchers, and continues to be an attractive and inspiring refuge for nature lovers from all over the world.

3 The Habitats of Bermuda

Although the island consists of a mere pinprick of land, one can find a large range of avian habitats, from remnants of the original, pre-colonial palmetto and cedar swamps to the urban centres and agricultural fields; from sandy beaches to sheer, crumbling limestone cliffs. A summary of each of the major habitat types, along with the more common attendant bird species, is given below.

The air

An often forgotten and neglected habitat, people tend to spend all their time peering intently into bushes and over ponds without looking up at the vast blue above them. Equal time should always be given to the skies, as it is here that the swallows and swifts skim past and vagrant raptors soar. Much of the migration also takes place above the islands, with many birds passing overhead at night without even stopping to rest on the island.

Open seas

Bermuda, sitting atop the remains of an underwater volcano, is surrounded by the Atlantic Ocean. This vast, glittering seascape of towering frothy waves and amethyst shallows is often overlooked by visitors who see it as an area for marine recreation but not for birding interest. Yet it is here that the pelagic migrants pass every year in their thousands, and the careful observer can spot several different species of shearwaters, jaegers, skuas and petrels from a comfortable perch on the shoreline. Good places to watch the pelagic migration include St David's Head and other select sites along the South Shore. The open seas around Bermuda also provide the hunting grounds for terns, the White-tailed Tropicbird (*Phaethon lepturus*) and the endemic cahow (*Pterodroma cahow*).

The coastline of South Shore

Although it is unlikely that one will see a cahow, your best bet is to scan the dusk skies over the Castle Islands during February to June, where a fast moving and ghostly shape may present itself. Or it may not!

Limestone cliffs

Bermuda's shoreline, while often gently sloping on to pink beaches and rolling dunes, occasionally overlooks high limestone cliffs. These soft and crumbling cliff faces are the nesting places for Bermuda's national bird, the White-tailed Tropicbird, known locally as the 'Longtail'. During the months of April to June, one can see the fluffy balls of down that comprise the longtail chicks, crouched hungrily in their nesting cavity, peering anxiously out for their parents to return with a mouthful of fish. Care should be taken to keep well clear of the chicks, as disturbance could result in the death or abandonment of the young. The cliffs of St David's Head and Spittal Pond are perfect areas for longtail watching. Unfortunately the cliff faces are increasingly becoming the home of large colonies

Limestone cliffs of South Shore

of introduced feral Rock Doves (*Columba livia*), whose raucous and messy habits have been suggested as a reason for the gradual retreat and disappearance of many of Bermuda's historical longtail colonies.

Offshore islands

Bermuda is actually an archipelago of over a 100 islands and although the five or six largest islands are joined together and constitute the 'mainland', the surrounding shallows are dotted with smaller outcrops of land. Some of these are little more than bare weathered limestone, while others are larger and covered with sparse vegetation including Bay Grapes (*Coccoloba uvifera*), Sea Ox-eye (*Borrichia arborescens*) and straggling Casuarinas (*Casuarina equisetifolia*). It is on some of these islands in Castle Harbour that the protected sanctuary of the cahow lies, while other islands have breeding pairs of Common Terns (*Sterna hirundo*) that vigorously defend their territory. These islands also serve as a refuge for vagrants and migrants and one can often spot cormorants and various tern and gull species resting on them.

Beaches and dunes

The pink beaches for which Bermuda is famous are not just the haunt of scantily clad sun worshippers. Sanderlings (*Calidris alba*) and Ruddy Turnstones (*Arenaria interpres*) can be seen during the migration, running one step ahead of the receding waves, hunting unlucky invertebrates. These are occasionally watched over by Yellow-crowned Night Herons (*Nyctanassa violacea*), which prowl the nearby vegetation for their favourite prey – land crabs. Gulls and terns glide and swoop over the beach and, further inshore, on the rolling dunes with their attendant scrub vegetation, weary migrant warblers, sparrows and various vagrants sit and call to one another. The dunes of Horseshoe Bay and other sections of the South Shore are excellent spots for birding forays.

Dune vegetation

Mudflats

There are several inland mudflats on the island, such as at Stocks Harbour, Spanish Point, Spittal Pond and Warwick Pond. These are criss-crossed with the lobate footprints of moorhens and coots and, during the migration, home to the probing forms of sandpipers, plovers and occasionally Black-necked Stilts (*Himantopus mexicanus*). Nearby stand herons and egrets, all watching intently for the ripples that betray unwary fish. These mudflats are often bordered by mangroves or large brackish ponds, which again provide further diverse habitats for other species.

Mangroves

The mangroves of Bermuda are the northernmost mangroves in the world and are located along the coast and further inland. On certain sections of the coastline (especially on the South Shore), one can find the fossilised remains of old mangroves, attesting to the shrinking nature of this habitat. Both Black (*Avicennia nitida*) and Red (*Rhizophora mangle*) mangroves contribute to this habitat in Bermuda, their aerial roots and sprawling masses providing home to invertebrates, breeding fish and, of course, attendant birds. Excellent

Black-necked Stilt

examples of mangroves can be seen at Hungry Bay and small patches at Riddle's Bay and Walsingham. These mangroves are the perfect place to find an array of migrant and vagrant warblers (especially Black-and-White Warblers (*Mniotilta varia*), Yellow Warblers (*Dendroica petechia*) and Northern Waterthrush (*Seiurus noveboracensis*)), as well as various herons and egrets.

Palmetto and cedar swamps, marshes and ponds

Before the first settlers, in pre-colonial times, Bermuda was covered with a dense, humid swamp composed mainly of Bermuda Palmetto (*Sabal bermudana*) and Bermuda Cedar (*Juniperus bermudiana*). This habitat can still be seen in the sprawling Paget Marsh, oddly located in the middle of a suburban area. This habitat holds an array of birdlife, including warblers, vireos, cardinals and sparrows in the bushes and shrubs, while moorhens, coots and herons patrol the winding channels and secret pools. Apart from this main swamp, other marshes and inland ponds can be found throughout the island, notably Spittal Pond, Stokes Point Nature Reserve and Devonshire Marsh. These again provide important birding habitat, and are hosts to flocks of ducks, teals, moorhens, waders and herons.

Spittal Pond

Red Phalarope in winter plumage on Spittal Pond

Woodlands

A vast majority of the island is covered in open woodlands. Unfortunately very little of this is now composed of native vegetation, although there are patches of Bermuda Cedar and Palmetto in localised areas. The majority of Bermuda's woodlands today are comprised of monocultures of Surinam Cherry (*Eugenia uniflora*), or mixtures of All-spice (*Pimneta officinallis*), Fiddlewood (*Citharexylum spinosum*) and Mexican Pepper (*Schinus terebinthifolius*). These introduced species have rapidly outcompeted most of the native species, but luckily they still provide refuge and food for the island's avifauna. Woodlands are the haunts of warblers, sparrows, vireos, vagrant passerines and raptors and the ubiquitous starlings. Good woodlands for birdwatching include Walsingham, Lagoon Park, Ferry Reach, St David's Head, Fort Scaur and the Arboretum.

Agricultural land

Despite Bermuda's small size, there is a large amount of agricultural land, in the shape of fields, pastures and small crops. This habitat is very important to a wide array of bird species, including

resident doves and sparrows as well as many migrant and vagrant passerines (such as thrushes, kingbirds and flycatchers) which hunt and hawk for insects in the fields. Migrant swallows and occasional swifts dart and skim above the fields in search of airborne insects and the more uncommon kestrels can sometimes be seen hovering above. After heavy rains, when the fields flood, waders begin to take an interest in the larger areas, stalking prey amidst the sodden grass tufts. Near the few cattle herds, one can often see Cattle Egrets (*Bubulcus ibis*) moving between bovine legs and among the pastures. There are several good farmland areas on the island, including the agricultural lands adjacent to Spittal Pond, Paget Marsh, Somerset Long Bay and Luke's Farm.

Garden of Bermudan stately home

Gardens

Bermuda from above looks like a giant suburb, dotted with the gleaming white roofs of houses and interspersed with patches of verdant green. The large gardens of many of Bermuda's stately homes, filled with a bewildering array of flowers from all corners of the globe, often attract passing migrants and vagrants. Many of the warbler, vireo and thrush species take an interest in the gardening efforts of Bermudians, as do local Eastern Bluebirds (*Sialia sialis*) and Bermuda White-eyed Vireos (*Vireo griseus bermudiensis*).

Urban areas

Sadly a large proportion of Bermuda consists of urban development, the ever-present human encroachments that are rapidly encompassing the globe. It is in this habitat of concrete and stone that one can find House Sparrows (*Passer domesticus*) and flocks of Starlings (*Sturnus vulgaris*). However, as most of Bermuda's large urban areas abut the sea, this results in occasional interesting finds in even the most dreary location. Hamilton and St George's often sport small gatherings of Ruddy Turnstones (*Arenaria interpres*) trotting along the docks and several gull species wheeling overhead, occasionally begging for scraps. These are often joined by waddling Mallards (*Anas platyrhynchos*), quacking and squabbling for bits of bread.

Open areas

Open grassy areas in Bermuda are generally found either on golf courses or at the airport. Golf courses are one of the most impor-

Upland Sandpiper

tant areas for breeding Eastern Bluebirds, with many nest boxes erected on the larger golf courses holding the gaping mouths of young bluebirds. It is here that one can obtain excellent views of hunting adults, as they struggle to gather enough food for their ravenous brood. Golf courses also provide perfect open habitat for a variety of waders (especially after heavy rains), swallows and swifts. Birders need to be ever watchful for projectile golf balls, and permission should be asked before entering the grounds. Riddell's Bay Golf Course, Port Royal and St George's Golf Club should provide good birding moments. The open flat grasslands surrounding the civil air terminal are incredibly important for an array of migrant and vagrant waders, and it is here that one has the best chances of seeing grassland species such as Killdeer (*Charadrius vociferus*), Black-bellied Plover (*Pluvialis squatarola*), Buff-breasted Sandpipers (*Tryngites subruficollis*) and Upland Sandpipers (*Bartramia longicauda*). These can even sometimes be seen from the roadside, if one peers through the fence at the flat land in front of the main terminal.

4 The Birds of Bermuda

At a superficial glance, Bermuda might seem to be a rather remote place to birdwatch. With most of the endemics long since extinct (due to a combination of early settlers eating them and an array of introduced species rapidly destroying the rest) and only 22 resident breeding species, it would seem that birdwatching in Bermuda would be distinctly unrewarding. Luckily nothing could be further from the truth!

Endemics

Bermuda has two endemics: the Bermuda White-eyed Vireo (*Vireo griseus bermudiensis*), which is a distinct sub-species of the American

Bermuda White-eyed Vireo

Cahow

White-eyed Vireo (*Vireo griseus griseus*), and the legendary Cahow (*Pterodroma cahow*). The cahow is a small petrel species that spends the majority of its time at sea, typically foraging in the Gulf Stream. The only time it comes to land is during the breeding season, with adults finding nesting sites in October and laying eggs in early February. The parents feed the chicks with squid plundered from the oceans, but eventually abandon their young to their own devices in late May. This forces the young to rapidly learn the secrets of flight with weeks of night-time exercising and flapping of wings. However, they too soon leave the island, to spend their first few years out at sea. The chances of actually seeing a cahow are exceptionally unlikely, as they nest on a handful of small offshore islands and only come in from their hunting forays at night. Despite the fact that a sighting would be very lucky indeed, the story of the cahow stirs the imagination and is one of the world's conservation success stories.

Before the infamous shipwreck in 1609 it was estimated that more than 2 million of these petrels made Bermuda their breeding ground, nesting in thousands of burrows on the ground. Unfortunately, being a bird that had never encountered any land-based threats before, they were exceptionally tame and were rapidly exterminated by the early settlers who could catch them with little effort to supplement their diet. Those that survived the initial onslaught were finished off by a combination of introduced wild pigs and rats. The cahow soon drifted off into the realms of history and was considered extinct. It was therefore a considerable surprise when a small breeding colony of the birds was discovered in the early 1950s on a small island in Castle Harbour. The colony was barely hanging on and was under considerable pressure from the White-tailed Tropicbirds, which also nest in the same cliffs and islands. Being far more aggressive, these birds were excluding cahows from their nesting sites and occasionally killing chicks.

The future, such as it was, looked tenuous at best. However, with the help and dedication of Dr David Wingate, the Chief Conservation Officer, the population began to increase, slowly but surely. One of the main salvations of the beleaguered population was the addition of a baffle in front of likely cahow burrows. This simple piece of wood reduced the size of the burrow's entrance, thus excluding marauding tropicbirds while allowing entrance to prospective cahow pairs. Despite several unexpected problems, such as the surprise appearance of a Snowy Owl (*Nyctea scandiaca*) in 1986 that managed to kill five adults in the space of a few weeks, the cahow has been brought back from the edge of extinction for a second time. In the recent 2003 breeding season, there were 70 established breedingh pairs that managed to fledge a record total of 40 young. This shows how successful these conservation initiatives have been. When management efforts commenced in earnest in 1962 there were only 18 pairs producing 8 fledgelings.

Although cahows present a serious birding challenge, Bermuda's second endemic is much more obliging. The Bermuda White-eyed Vireo is a small, inquisitive, plump vireo that is a common denizen of woodlands, mangroves, parklands and other shrubby areas. It can be easily found as it hops about in the trees and bushes, and responds well to 'pishing'. It can also be located by its distinctive call, which sounds like 'Chick-of-the-village'; this has earned it its local name.

Natives

Of the 22 resident species, only half of these (including the two endemics) have reached the island by natural means. Of these, two

Common Tern (juvenile)

White-tailed Tropicbird

are sea-birds: the Common Tern (*Sterna hirundo*) and the White-tailed Tropicbird. Approxmately 20 pairs of Common Terns breed on small islands off the mainland (especially the Castle Islands), where they aggressively protect their young from all intruders. Small flocks of Common Terns can often be seen in the harbours and bays dive-bombing schools of fish that stray too close to the water's surface. The Castle Islands are also a good place to see tropicbirds when they return to breed. In March, the cliffs and coastlines of Bermuda are host to thousands of these beautiful and graceful birds, as they set about raising their chicks after months out at sea.

The majority of native species are, however, land birds. Throughout the island the bushes ring with the cat-like calls of Grey Catbirds (*Dumetella carolinensis*) and the soft cooing of Mourning Doves (*Zenaida macroura*) and Common Ground Doves (*Columbina passerina*). On the more open areas of the island (especially golf courses), one can see pairs of Eastern Bluebirds feeding their young in strategically placed nest boxes. Bermuda is the only place outside of mainland North America where this species breeds. These birds were hit heavily by a combination of factors: chiefly the destruction of their nesting sites in native cedar trees by the cedar blight in the 1940s; the appearance of DDT in the food chain; and the introduction of house sparrows and starlings. After an intensive, island-wide campaign of providing the birds with nest boxes in which to raise their young, the birds are beginning to make a come-back. Golf courses and other open areas are also the best places at dusk to observe the ghostly forms of hunting Barn Owls (*Tyto alba*), of which there are several breeding pairs on the island.

The native birds are rounded off by Common Moorhens (*Gallinula chloropus*) and American Coots (*Fulica americana*), both of which breed in marshes and ponds. They can often be spotted paddling lazily about with a line of fuzzy chicks trailing behind.

Introductions

Like most islands, Bermuda has been inundated with a large number of introductions; indeed over half of the island's resident birds are alien species. Some of these introductions were relatively benign and the deliberate introduction or escapes of various cage birds have led to an injection of colour to the island's native avifauna. Species such as the Cardinal (*Cardinalis cardinalis*), with the vivid scarlet feathers of the males, and the European Goldfinch (*Carduelis carduelis*) appeared on the island in the distant past and have become accepted features of the island's bird life. Their impact as competitors on native species is minimal. Other species, such as the Orange-cheeked Waxbill (*Estrilda melopoda*) and Common Waxbill (*Estrilda astrild*), are present in such small numbers that they are not considered a threat to any of the native species.

The deliberate introduction of the Yellow-crowned Night Heron (*Nyctanassa violacea*) was also carried out as an attempt to reverse the imbalance of land crabs caused by the extinction of an endemic night heron in early colonial days. This bird acted as their chief predator and, with its disappearance, the crab populations flourished to the point where native vegetation was becoming damaged. The Yellow-crowned Night Heron is similar in almost every respect to this extinct endemic and may itself have nested on the island during pre-colonial times. Its introduction was very successful and numerous birds can now be seen roosting at several of the island's nature reserves (Spittal Pond being a prime area for observing clusters of these gorgeous birds). The sad remains of their invertebrate prey can be found scattered over the rocky shorelines of Bermuda, thus bringing the crab population explosion back into balance.

Unfortunately, as is true the world over, benign introductions are the exception and not the rule in Bermuda. A classic example is the Great Kiskadee (*Pitangus sulphuratus*), an introduction from Trinidad. This member of the tyrant flycatchers is a large, aggressive species, brought into the island to control *Anolis* lizards (which, in a classic display of humanity's penchant for making a bad situation worse, had been introduced to the island to control cockroaches). Today, the kiskadee is much in evidence, its sulphur yellow breast and black and white head pouring forth the scolding 'Kis-ka-dee' call. Unfortunately, instead of preying solely on *Anolis* species, it has taken to hunting the endemic Bermuda Rock Lizard (*Eumeces longirostros*) as well as the nestlings of many native bird species (including bluebirds). Another introduction, the American Crow (*Corvus brachyrhynchos*) rapidly established itself in Bermuda and huge flocks are now a common sight on the island. Interestingly, several pairs of crows have learned how to hunt longtail chicks, hovering down the sides of cliffs and pulling the chicks to their doom.

This predation on native species is not the only problem caused by introductions. The House Sparrow (*Passer domesticus*), a famil-

6 Birdwatching

Birdwatching is a fascinating and rewarding pastime and is rapidly expanding throughout the world as a leading force behind ecotourism and conservation. However, birdwatching can also be exceptionally frustrating if one doesn't have the appropriate equipment or the basic knowledge. This chapter aims to provide the novice birder with the basics to aid in making birdwatching a pleasant and exciting experience.

Basic bird identification

While one doesn't need to know the technical and scientific jargon associated with bird anatomy, it is important to become familiar with those parts of the bird that are commonly used in identification. A knowledge of the following terms, in conjunction with Figure 1 on page 40, will aid in bird identification:

◆ Head

- **Upper and lower mandible** – top and bottom of the beak or bill.
- **Cere** – in raptors, the leathery saddle at the base of the upper mandible.
- **Frontal shield** – in coots and moorhens, a flat extension of the bill on the forehead.
- **Lore** – area between the beak and the eye
- **Supercilium** or **eyebrow** – stripe located above the eye.
- **Eye stripe** – stripe located through the eye.
- **Moustachial stripe** – stripe running down the side of the cheek.
- **Malar stripe** – stripe running down the side of the throat.

◆ Wings

- **Wing bar(s)** – stripe or stripes located in the middle of the wing.
- **Primary feathers** – large feathers on the trailing edge of the wing, from tip of wing to bend caused by wrist.

Parts of a Bird

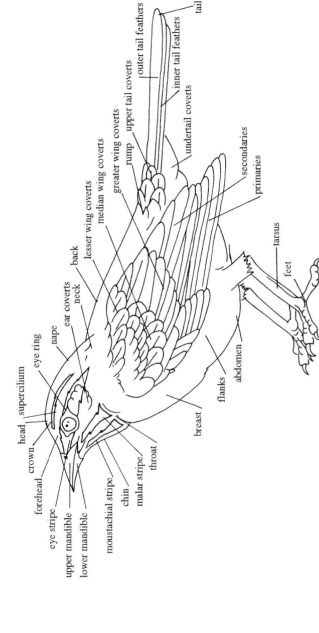

Figure 1. Diagram showing relevant bird terminology

- **Secondary feathers** – large feathers on the trailing edge of the wing, from end of primary feathers to body.
- **Wing coverts** – small feathers on wing that cover the primaries and secondaries at point where they connect to the bone.
- **Leading edge** – front edge of wing, when bird is seen in flight.
- **Trailing edge** – back edge of wing, when bird is seen in flight.
- **Speculum** – in ducks, a section of brightly coloured primary feathers on the trailing edge of the wing.

As well as learning these basic terms, it is also important to be aware of the main areas of the bird that need to be carefully observed in order to obtain a satisfactory identification. Areas of importance include: the **throat** (whether it is clear, striped, spotted, etc.); the **breast** (whether it is clear, striped, spotted, mottled, etc.); and the **colour**, both overall and that of the leg, eye, back and breast. The presence of defining marks is also important, such as wing bars, coloured speculums, head striping, speckling, obvious crests and plumes, etc.

It is a simple fact that you are unlikely to identify every single bird you see. However, by going out into the field armed with the knowledge of likely species or families in the area and by making frequent birding forays, your knowledge and level of understanding will increase dramatically.

The science of birdwatching

Knowing the anatomy of birds, and knowing the common species and families is just part of the process. Careful planning of your trip will also lead to good sightings and maximise your time in the field.

◆ Some key pointers to birdwatching

- Choose appropriate times of day for birdwatching. Although it is possible, during the correct time of year, to watch pelagic migrants all day long, most land birds and migrants will be most active at dawn and dusk. By going out into the field early in the morning or late in the afternoon, you will be far more likely to see a variety of birds than if you were to go out at the height of the midday sun.
- Maximise the number of habitats you visit in a single trip. If you spend all your time birding in woodlands, then you will severely cut down the number of species you could see. Instead, visit a

couple of ponds, a mangrove, the coastline and a golf course as well as woodlands, and your success rate will be much higher.

- Check the time of year that you are birding and become familiar with the species you are likely to see. If it is April or October, for example, make special trips to mangroves for migrant warblers, or to mudflats to find waders and ducks. If it is May, visit the North Shore to scan the sea for pelagic migrants. By being aware of the time of year that birds are likely to appear you won't miss migrations that make birding in Bermuda so exciting.

- Make detailed notes of the birds you see, especially if you are a novice to birdwatching. This means noting down as much information as possible about the bird, from overall colour to information on markings, crests, plumes, colour of the legs, etc. This serves several purposes. Firstly, it allows you to check at your leisure for the identification of a bird you have seen, especially if there are several birds that are similar. Secondly, by keeping notes on the birds you see you can start to get an idea of the overall ebb and flow of birds through Bermuda. By looking at notes of birds seen in previous years, you can then be ready for them at the appropriate time next year.

- Gradually build up an idea of the best places to birdwatch in your area. This means that you won't waste time going to areas with little action and can concentrate your time on areas where the chances of getting a good sighting are highest. Many avid birdwatchers have their own 'patch' or route that they follow on a regular basis in order to obtain the maximum number of interesting sightings.

Binoculars

All of the above advice and information is almost useless if you don't have the proper equipment with you. There can be nothing more frustrating than trying to birdwatch with a pair of binoculars that costs $5 (£3) and has a view field the size of a thimble. It is well worth paying the extra money for a decent pair of binoculars that will last for many years.

The most important considerations when deciding what binoculars you should buy are:

- **The magnification of the binoculars.** All binoculars have two numbers on them, the magnification and the diameter of the objective lens, displayed as 8 × 40 (for example). The first number, the magnification, means how many times an object is magnified through the binoculars. If the binoculars have a magnification of 8, then something that is 80 metres away will in fact appear as if it is only 10 metres away. Large magnifications bring the object closer, but also serve to magnify the shaking of your hand. It is therefore advisable to buy a pair of binoculars with a magnification of 7 or 8 as this should be sufficient for identification without causing too many difficulties.

- **The diameter of the objective lens.** This is the second number on the binoculars and indicates how wide the lens is at the far end of the binoculars. The larger the diameter, the more light the binoculars will let in, and the better your binoculars will be when used in dim light conditions. A good rule of thumb is to be able to divide the diameter of the objective lens by five to obtain your magnification (i.e. 7 × 35, 8 × 40, 10 × 50). This provides the optimum levels of magnification matched with amount of incoming light levels.
- **Waterproof/weatherproof.** Although it is good to have binoculars that are waterproof, it is not essential and does serve to increase the price of binoculars dramatically. However, if you are buying the binoculars as a long-term investment, then waterproofing should be seriously considered. If your binoculars are not waterproof then you must be sure to take extra care of them when out in the field (take precautions such as always keeping a waterproof bag on you in case of sudden showers).
- **Weight.** Try to buy a pair of binoculars that is as light as possible, because you do not want something very heavy hanging around your neck! A lighter pair of binoculars will make birding more enjoyable and less stressful after a long day in the field.

Finally, a note on spotting scopes. If you are serious about birdwatching and want to get a positive identification on the huddled forms of sandpipers on a distant mudflat, then you might want to consider buying a spotting scope. This of course has pros and cons. On the negative side, scopes are expensive and it means that you have to carry an extra, bulky piece of equipment around with you. However, on the plus side, it means that you now have powers of magnification impossible in standard binoculars and will thus be able to pick out clearly the dark shapes of shearwaters skimming over the ocean waves from the shoreline.

7 The Birds of Bermuda: Species Listings

This chapter contains full accounts of the more common species found in Bermuda, along with all the resident species and the two endemics. As there are over 350 species that can be found on the island at different times of the year, it is not feasible to fully describe each species. For a full list of all species found in Bermuda, refer to the checklist found in Chapter 1, which includes abundance ratings and island status (i.e. Resident, Migrant, Vagrant, etc.).

Each species described on the following pages is treated in the following way. The common name, or names, is given along with the scientific name. Scientific names are important as they allow readers from different countries where the species may have different common names to ascertain exactly which species is being discussed.

The length of the bird, taken from the tip of the beak to the tip of the tail, is given in both inches and centimetres. The length of the bird is often very important in species identification and a rough estimation of the bird's length should always be made while in the field.

Identification is made using the most distinctive parts of the plumage, eye colours, legs, feet, etc. Bird identification can be very difficult in many species, but by taking into account all details of the bird in question, species can be identified by a process of elimination. If there are dimorphic differences (i.e. males and females have different plumages), then these are referred to, as are differences in breeding condition and immature plumages. It is important to note that many of the bird species that visit the island will never be in breeding plumage, as they are merely on passage to, or from, breeding sites.

The habitat designations used in this guide are quite broad, and the absence of a habitat from the bird account does not mean that the species will never be found in that habitat. Habitat designations merely refer to the habitats where you are most likely to find the species in Bermuda.

Similar species includes those species with which the bird may be most confused. These are only other birds recorded from Bermuda and not all species with which there could be confusion (i.e. Eastern Bluebird (*Sialia sialis*) could be confused with Western Bluebird (*Sialia mexicana*) but because the latter species has never been recorded in Bermuda, this is not mentioned). Identification tips for distinguishing problem species are then provided to allow comparison between similar species. If there are no other species with which the bird in question may be confused, then it is merely listed as *Distinctive*.

Finally the status of the bird in Bermuda is given. This rating (in decreasing abundance from Abundant, Common, Frequent, Uncommon, Occasional and Rare) denotes how likely you are to encounter the species while birdwatching in Bermuda. Status and designation are more fully explained in Chapter 1. It is important to remember that the abundance rating only corresponds to the relevant time of year.

A total of 132 species are given full species accounts on the following pages.

Family Podicipedidae (Grebes)

(Total recorded: 4 species – Migrant 1 sp., Vagrant 3 spp.)

◆ 6. Pied-billed Grebe   *Podilymbus podiceps*

Length: 13 inches (33 cm)

Identification: A small brown grebe found singly and in pairs. Upperparts chocolate brown, underparts paler brown and mottled. Head and neck rufous, throat white. Thick pale bill and white undertail coverts. *Breeding* birds acquire a black ring on the bill, while the pale rufous throat and white chin become black. Sexes alike. *Immatures* are similar in coloration to winter birds, but have a brown and white streaked head and neck.

Habitat: Ponds, marshes and shallow bays.

Similar species: Distinctive.

Status: Common migrant with recent breeding records.

Pied-billed Grebe: adult, left; immature, right

Family Procellariidae (Petrels, Shearwaters, Storm Petrels, Prions)

(Total recorded: 7 species – Endemic 1 sp., Pelagic 5 spp., Vagrant 1 sp.)

◆ 8. Greater Shearwater   *Puffinus gravis*

Length: 19 inches (48 cm)

Identification: A large shearwater seen on migration off the coast of Bermuda. Dark grey-brown above and white below with a distinctive dark brown cap. Black tail with a thin, white, crescent-shaped rump patch. Sexes alike.

Habitat: Atlantic Ocean, breeding mainly on Tristan de Cunha Island in the South Atlantic.

Similar species: Cory's Shearwater (*Calonectris diomedea*), which it often joins in migration, but which lacks the dark head cap and white rump patch.

Status: Abundant pelagic migrant.

◆ 10. Manx Shearwater   *Puffinus puffinus*

Length: 13 inches (33 cm)

Identification: A small shearwater, encountered on migration off the coast of Bermuda. Black above and white below, with white underwings and under tail. Tail does not extend beyond feet. Sexes alike.

Habitat: Atlantic Ocean, breeding in Mexico, Hawaii and small islands off the coast of Europe.

Similar species: Audubon's Shearwater (*Puffinus lherminieri*), which has a *longer* tail (extending beyond the legs) and *white* cheeks.

Status: Common pelagic migrant.

◆ 12. Cahow (Bermuda Petrel)   *Pterodroma cahow*

Length: 15 inches (38 cm)

Identification: A medium-sized dark grey and white petrel. Head has a black cap with a white forehead. Belly and vent white, tail black with a conspicuous pale rump patch. Sexes alike.

Habitat: Atlantic Ocean, only coming ashore to Bermuda to breed.

Similar species: Black-capped Petrel (*Pterodroma hasitata*), which has a *white collar* and *white* rump. Audubon's Shearwater (*Puffinus lherminieri*), which is a smaller black *and white* seabird with a *black* rump.

Status: Endemic, rare resident (in breeding season: October–June).

Family Phaethontidae (Tropicbirds)

(Total recorded: 2 species – Resident (seasonal) 1 sp., Vagrant 1 sp.)

◆ 18. White-tailed Tropicbird (Longtail)   *Phaethon lepturus*

Length: 32 inches (80 cm)

Identification: A very distinctive white and black seabird with two long white tail streamers (up to 16 inches (40 cm) long). Bill yellow to orange-red. Sexes alike. *Immatures* lack the tail streamers, have a yellow bill and are heavily streaked and barred with black.

Immature Tropicbird on nest

Habitat: Pantropical oceans, with Bermuda being its northernmost breeding grounds.

Similar species: Red-billed Tropicbird (*Phaethon aethereus*), a very rare vagrant to Bermuda, which has a *red bill* and *heavily barred* black and white back and wings.

Status: Abundant resident (in breeding season: late February to late October).

Family Phalacrocoracidae (Cormorants)

(Total recorded: 2 species – Vagrant 2 spp.)

◆ 24. Double-crested Cormorant   *Phalacrocorax auritus*

Length: 33 inches (83 cm)

Identification: A large black cormorant with a conspicuous orange throat patch. *Breeding* birds have a double crest of white feathers

Double-crested Cormorant

originating behind the eyes and curving over the back of the head. *Immature* birds are brown above with a pale upper breast and neck. Sexes alike.

Habitat: Coast, offshore islands and sheltered bays.

Similar species: Great Cormorant (*Phalacrocorax carbo*), which is slightly larger and has *white* cheeks and chin and a *yellow* throat pouch.

Status: Common vagrant.

Family Ardeidae (Herons, Egrets and Bitterns)

(Total recorded: 12 species – Introduced 1 sp., Migrant 1 sp., Vagrant 10 spp.)

◆ 25. Great Blue Heron   *Ardea herodias*

Length: 46 inches (117 cm)

Identification: a very large grey-blue heron with a pale grey neck and black and white throat. A prominent black stripe extends from

Great Blue Heron

the eye over the back of the head. The large, dagger-like bill is yellow and the thighs are rufous brown. Sexes alike. *Breeding* birds acquire plumes on the head, neck and back.

Habitat: Mangroves, ponds, marshes and coast.

Similar species: The large size distinguishes this species from all other grey-blue herons.

Status: Common migrant.

◆ 26. Green Heron   *Butorides striatus*

Length: 18 inches (46 cm)

Identification: A small stocky heron with blue-grey back and chestnut neck. Head has a green-black cap with white throat and neck. Legs are short and dull yellow. *Immatures* are brown with heavily streaked brown and white throat and underparts. Sexes alike.

Habitat: Marshes, swamps, ponds and mangroves.

Similar species: Adults distinctive. Immatures could be confused with immature Yellow-crowned Night Herons (*Nyctanassa violacea*), which are *larger* and *lack* the faded green-black cap.

Status: Common vagrant with recent breeding records.

Green Heron

◆ 27. Little Blue Heron　　　　　*Egretta caerulea*

Length: 24 inches (61 cm)

Identification: A medium-sized, slender heron with a slate grey body and maroon neck and head. Legs and beak black. *Breeding* birds have reddish purple neck and plumes on the crown, back and neck. *Immatures* are pure white with dull olive legs and feet and a pale blue bill tipped with black. Sexes alike.

Habitat: Marshes, ponds and shorelines.

Similar species: Adult could be confused with Louisiana Heron (*Egretta tricolor*), which has a *white* belly and *white* throat. Juveniles could be confused with any of the egret species, but the combination of dull olive legs and feet and pale blue bill should prevent misidentification.

Status: Frequent vagrant.

Little Blue Heron: juvenile on Spittal Pond

◆ 28. Tricolored Heron   *Egretta tricolor*

Length: 26 inches (65 cm)

Identification: A medium-sized dark blue heron with a conspicuous white belly, rump and throat. *Immatures* have a chestnut back and chestnut mottling on grey-blue wings. Sexes alike.

Habitat: Marshes, ponds and shorelines.

Similar species: Little Blue Heron (*Egretta caerulea*), which *lacks* the white belly and throat and has a *maroon* head and neck.

Status: Frequent vagrant.

Tricolored Heron

Snowy Egret on Spittal Pond

 29. Snowy Egret *Egretta thula*

Length: 24 inches (61 cm)

Identification: a medium-sized white heron with slender black bill, black legs and yellow feet. *Breeding* birds acquire elegant recurved plumes on the head, neck and back and the lores and feet turn bright red. Sexes alike.
Habitat: Marshes, ponds, mangroves and shorelines.
Similar species: The combination of black bill, black legs and yellow feet distinguish this species from all other similarly plumaged herons.
Status: Frequent vagrant.

 31. Cattle Egret *Bubulcus ibis*

Length: 20 inches (50 cm)

Identification: A small, stocky white heron with a thick blunt yellow bill and yellow-green legs. *Breeding* birds acquire a buff wash

Cattle Egret showing breeding plumage

to the feathers of the crown, neck and back, while the bill and legs
turn orange-pink. Sexes alike.

Habitat: Marshes, ponds, fields and agricultural land.

Similar species: The buff wash of breeding birds distinguishes the
species from all other similarly plumaged herons. Non-breeding
adults could be confused with juvenile Little Blue Herons (*Egretta
caerulea*), which have a more slender, *bluish* beak and are *less stocky*.

Status: Common vagrant.

◆ 32. Great Egret   *Casmerodius albus*

Length: 38 inches (95 cm)

Identification: A large white heron with a large yellow bill. Legs
and feet black. *Breeding* birds acquire long straight plumes which
emerge from the back and trail over the tail. Sexes alike.

Habitat: Marshes, ponds, mangroves and shorelines.

Similar species: The large size distinguishes this species from all
other similarly plumaged herons.

Status: Frequent vagrant.

Great Egret

Yellow-crowned Night Heron with crab

◆ 34. Yellow-crowned Night Heron *Nyctanassa violacea*

Length: 24 inches (61 cm)

Identification: A medium-sized pale grey heron, often in large groups (especially when roosting). Conspicuous black head with white cheek patches and white crown, flushed with yellow. Red eyes. *Breeding* birds acquire tufted feathers at the back of the head. *Immatures* are a dull brown, finely speckled with white. Sexes alike.

Habitat: Marshes, swamps, ponds and mangroves.

Similar species: Immatures resemble adult American Bittern (*Botaurus lentiginosus*), which has *black* throat stripes, black outer wing feathers and a *yellow* eye. Black-crowned Night Heron (*Nycticorax nycticorax*) adults have a *black* back and *black* cap; immatures have a *paler brown* striped breast and a *darker brown* back, *heavily* spotted with white.

Status: Common resident.

◆ 36. American Bittern *Botaurus lentiginosus*

Length: 23 inches (58 cm)

Identification: A medium sized, stocky heron with cryptic brown and white coloration. At rest, with bill pointing upwards, conspicuous black neck stripes are revealed. *In flight* black outer wing feathers become apparent. Sexes alike. *Immatures* lack black neck stripes.

Habitat: Ponds, fields and marshes.

Similar species: Could be confused with juvenile Yellow-crowned Night Heron (*Nyctanassa violacea*) which *lacks* black throat stripes and black outer wing feathers, and has white spots on upper wings and a *red* eye.

Status: Uncommon vagrant.

Family Threskiornithidae (Ibises and Spoonbills)

(Total recorded: 2 species – Vagrant 2 spp.)

◆ 37. Glossy Ibis   *Plegadis falcinellus*

Length: 23 inches (58 cm)

Identification: A medium-sized ibis with uniform glossy purple plumage and a long decurved bill. Bill and legs black. *Immatures are a dull olive brown with a paler bill.* Sexes alike.
Habitat: Marshes, fields and ponds.
Similar species: Distinctive.
Status: Uncommon vagrant.

Family Anatidae (Ducks and Geese)

(Total recorded: 36 species – Resident 1 sp., Migrant 1 sp., Vagrant 34 spp.)

◆ 43. Canada Goose   *Branta canadensis*

Length: 34 inches (76 cm)

Identification: A large brown goose with a black head and neck. A distinctive white 'chinstrap' extends up the side of the head. The black tail is preceded by a pure white rump, with white undertail feathers. Sexes alike.
Habitat: Ponds, marshes, fields, agricultural land and golf courses.
Similar species: Distinctive.
Status: Frequent vagrant.

◆ 45. Snow Goose   *Chen caerulescens*

Length: 28 inches (71 cm)

Identification: A medium-sized white goose with pink bill and feet. Primaries are black. A rarer 'blue' colour phase has a white head and neck, brown back and belly with varying amounts of white mottling. *Immatures are mottled pale grey with a dark grey bill.* Sexes alike.

Snow Goose

Habitat: Marshes, ponds, fields, agricultural land and golf courses.
Similar species: Distinctive.
Status: Frequent vagrant.

◆ 49. Mallard   *Anas platyrhynchos*
Length: 23 inches (58 cm)

Identification: A large, familiar dabbling duck which, due to domestic breeding, can have several different colour phases. Only the standard plumage will be described. *In flight* has a distinctive metallic blue speculum. *Males* have a metallic green head, white collar and chestnut chest. Body is grey and brown and rump black and white. *Females* are brown with a yellow beak, blue speculum bordered with white and a white tail.
Habitat: Lakes, ponds, marshes, coast, docks, fields and agricultural land.
Similar species: Male distinctive. Females could be confused with American Black Ducks (*Anas rubripes*) with which it hybridises; Males have a *chocolate brown* body and *pale brown* head. Females have a blue speculum *without* white borders.
Status: Introduced, common resident and uncommon vagrant.

Mallard ♂

Mallard ♀ with chicks

◆ 50. American Black Duck   *Anas rubripes*

Length: 23 inches (62 cm)

Identification: A large dark chocolate brown duck with a deep purple speculum. The head is pale grey-brown with chocolate brown on the crown and a thin chocolate brown eye stripe. *Males* have a yellow bill, *females* have a dull green bill. *In flight* shows deep purple speculum, bordered black and with a faint white trailing edge.
Habitat: Ponds and marshes.
Similar species: Could be confused with female Mallard, which has a purple speculum *bordered white* and is a much *lighter* brown.
Status: Frequent vagrant.

◆ 53. Green-winged Teal   *Anas crecca*

Length: 14 inches (35 cm)

Identification: A small dabbling duck found singly, in pairs and occasionally in small flocks. *In flight* shows a distinctive irridescent green speculum. *Males* have pale grey bodies, pinkish breasts bordered by a thin white vertical line and a distinctive chestnut and dark green head. Rump is pale yellow and black. *Females* are pale mottled brown, with a buff undertail and prominent green speculum even at rest.
Habitat: Lakes, ponds and marshes.
Similar species: Male distinctive. Females can be confused with other female dabblers, especially Blue-winged Teals (*Anas discors*), but its small size and green speculum should prevent misidentification.
Status: Frequent vagrant.

◆ 54. Blue-winged Teal   *Anas discors*

Length: 16 inches (40 cm)

Identification: A small dabbling duck found singly and in small flocks. *In flight* has a distinctive pale blue shoulder patch and green speculum. *Males* are brown with a grey head showing a large, white vertical crescent-shaped mark between the eye and beak. Rump is black and white. *Females* are pale mottled brown with pale blue shoulders and a green speculum.
Habitat: Lakes, ponds and marshes.

Blue-winged Teal

Similar species: Male distinctive. Females can be confused with other female dabblers, especially Green-winged Teals (*Anas crecca*), but the *pale blue* shoulder should prevent misidentification.
Status: Common migrant.

◆ 57. American Wigeon   *Anas americana*

Length: 19 inches (48 cm)

Identification: A medium-sized dabbling duck found singly, in pairs or in small flocks. *In flight* has distinctive white shoulders and green speculum. *Males* have a grey and green head with a prominent white crown. Body is brown and rump black and white. *Females* have a grey-brown head, brown back and chest and white belly. The green speculum can sometimes be seen on folded wings.
Habitat: Lakes, ponds and marshes.
Similar species: Males distinctive. Females could be confused with other female dabbling ducks, but the white shoulders and green speculum should prevent misidentification.
Status: Uncommon vagrant.

American Wigeon

◆ 62. Ring-necked Duck *Aythya collaris*

Length: 17 inches (43 cm)

Identification: A small diving duck found singly, in pairs or small flocks. *Males* have a black breast, back and tail, grey sides and deep purple head with yellow eye. A distinctive white vertical stripe separates black breast from grey sides. Grey bill has a white ring separating black tip. Thin white line between bill and purple head. *Females* are chocolate brown with black eye, white eye ring and white ring on black tipped, grey bill.

Habitat: Lakes, ponds and marshes.

Similar species: Males could be confused with: (i) male Greater Scaup (*Aythya marila*), which has a *metallic green* head, *grey* back and *lacks* the white ring on the beak; (ii) male Lesser Scaup (*Aythya affinis*), which has a *grey* back and *lacks* the white ring on the beak. Females could be confused with female scaups, which are darker and have a distinctive white facial patch before the bill.

Status: Frequent vagrant.

◆ **64. Canvasback**   *Aythya valisineria*

Length: 21 inches (53 cm)

Identification: A large diving duck found singly or in pairs. *Males* have a pale grey back, white belly, black breast and chestnut head and neck, red eyes, long black bill and black rump. *Females* are grey-brown, with pale brown neck and black eyes.
Habitat: Lakes, ponds and marshes.
Similar species: Redhead (*Aythya americana*). Males have a *shorter*, *grey* bill *tipped* with *black* and *black* eyes. Females have *brown* head, neck, back and belly and a grey bill *tipped with black*.
Status: Uncommon vagrant.

◆ **66. Lesser Scaup**   *Aythya affinis*

Length: 16.5 inches (42 cm)

Identification: A medium sized diving duck with a slight pointed head. *Males* have a deep purple head and a black neck, breast and tail. Back is grey and belly and sides white. *Females* are chocolate brown, becoming lighter on sides, and have a prominent white patch on the face before the beak. *In flight* shows large white patch on secondaries, with primary feathers a light grey.
Habitat: Ponds and marshes.
Similar species: Easily confused with Greater Scaup, which is larger and has a rounded head. Males have a dark green head, which is hard to discern in poor light conditions. Female has a darker head and neck. Ring-necked Duck is also similar, but both sexes have distinctive white band on the bill. Tufted Duck shares similar colour patterns, but has a conspicuous tuft of feathers extending off the back of the head.
Status: Uncommon vagrant.

◆ **67. Common Goldeneye**   *Bucephala clangula*

Length: 20 inches (50 cm)

Identification: A medium-sized diving duck, usually solitary. Rounded head and small, grey bill. *Males* have a white breast, neck and sides and a black back and tail. The head is metallic green with a round white patch in front of the bill. *Females* have a grey body with a white collar and brown head. White wing patches are conspicuous in flight.

Habitat: Lakes, ponds and marshes.
Similar species: Barrow's Goldeneye (*Bucephala islandica*), currently unconfirmed on the species list for the island. Males have a *metallic purple* head and a *crescent-shaped* white patch on the head. Females normally have a more orange coloured bill.
Status: Uncommon vagrant.

◆ 68. Bufflehead   *Bucephala albeola*

Length: 14 inches (35 cm)

Identification: A very small diving duck with a rounded head, found singly or in pairs. *Males* have white breast, neck and sides, a black back and grey tail. The head is deep green-purple with a large helmet-like white patch on the back. *Females* are grey-brown with a white neck and brown head. Head has conspicuous white cheek patch.
Habitat: Lakes, ponds and marshes.
Similar species: Males could be confused with: (i) male Common Goldeneye (*Bucephala clangula*) which are *larger* and *lack* the white helmet patch; (ii) male Hooded Merganser (*Lophodytes cucullatus*) which has *chestnut* sides and a large white head patch *bordered with black*. Females could be confused with both of the female Goldeneyes, but both *lack* the white cheek patch.
Status: Occasional vagrant.

◆ 74. Hooded Merganser   *Lophodytes cucullatus*

Length: 18 inches (47 cm)

Identification: A very distinctive diving duck with a hammer-head appearance and thin, serrated bill. *Males* have a black head with a large white patch on the sides, and a white neck with a single black band and black edging. Wings, back and tail black, sides and belly pale brown. *Females* are pale grey-brown with white wing patches. *In flight* shows black and white patch on primaries. It is important to note that the crest is flattened in flight.
Habitat: Ponds and marshes.
Similar species: The combination of large hammer-head crest and black, white and brown colours makes the male distinctive. Females could be confused with female Red-breasted Merganser, but they are much *larger* and have a *dishevelled* appearance to their crest.
Status: Occasional vagrant.

◆ 76. Red-breasted Merganser   *Mergus serrator*

Length: 23 inches (58 cm)

Identification: A large diving duck found singly, in pairs or in small flocks. Conspicuous long, red bill with serrated edges. *Males* have a black back, grey and white sides, pale brown and black streaked breast and a white neck. The head is dark green with a prominent crest. *Females* are grey with a pale orange-brown head and prominent crest.
Habitat: In Bermuda always on inshore waters.
Similar species: Common Merganser (*Mergus merganser*): males have a *white* breast and *white* sides, females have a *prominent white throat patch* and a *distinct* demarcation between brown neck and grey-white body.
Status: Uncommon vagrant.

Family Rallidae (Rails, Gallinules and Coots)

(Total recorded: 9 species – Resident 2 spp., Vagrant 7 spp.)

◆ 79. Sora Rail   *Porzana carolina*

Length: 9 inches (23 cm)

Identification: A medium-sized, plump rail found singly or in pairs. Dark olive brown back, tail and wings, streaked with white and black. Brown capped, pale grey head with black chin, lore and throat. Bright yellow bill, red eye and yellow legs. Upper breast grey, lower breast buff brown with prominent white bars. Sexes alike. *Immatures* lack the pale grey head and breast of the adult, as well as the black chin, lore and throat.
Habitat: Marshes, swamps, ponds and mangroves.
Similar species: Yellow rail (*Coturnicops noveboracensis*) resembles immature, but is *smaller* with *yellowish* streaking above and *conspicuous white wing* patches in flight. Corn crake (*Crex crex*) resembles immature, but has *black* eyes and *red-brown* wings. Virginia rail (*Rallus limicola*) has a *long, red* bill, *rufous* breast and *red* legs. Immature Purple Gallinule (*Porphyrula martinica*) has a *pale yellow* bill and *lacks* the barring on the belly. Immature Common Moorhen (*Gallinula chloropus*) has a *pale yellow* bill, *white* band on flanks and *lacks* the barring on the belly.
Status: Frequent vagrant.

Sora Rail

◆ 84. Common Gallinule (Moorhen) *Gallinula chloropus*

Length: 13 inches (33 cm)

Identification: A medium sized gallinule found singly, in pairs or in small flocks. Chocolate brown back, wings and tail. Head and neck dark grey, breast and belly pale grey. Beak bright red with a yellow tip and a distinctive bright red frontal shield. Flanks have a prominent white band. Undertail coverts conspicuously white. Sexes alike. *Immatures* paler in coloration, with pale bill and frontal shield.

Habitat: Marshes, ponds, lakes, fields and golf courses.

Similar species: Purple Gallinule (*Porphyrula martinica*) which has a *metallic, purple-green* head, neck and breast, *pale blue* frontal shield and conspicuous *white* rump. Immatures *lack* white band on flank. American Coot (*Fulica americana*) is *dark grey* and has a *white* bill and frontal shield.

Status: Common resident and migrant.

Common Gallinule (Moorhen)

American Coot

◆ 85. American Coot

Fulica americana

Length: 15 inches (38 cm)

Identification: A large, slaty grey coot found singly, in pairs or small flocks. Eyes red and legs green-yellow. Bill is white with a distinctive white frontal shield. Head is darker grey when compared with the rest of the body. Undertail has a white patch divided by central dark grey feathers. Sexes alike. *Immatures* are paler and more washed-out than adults, especially on the head and neck.
Habitat: Marshes, ponds, lakes, fields and golf courses.
Similar species: Common Moorhen (*Gallinula chloropus*) which has a *bright red* frontal shield and *bright red-orange* beak. Back and tail are *brown* and there is a distinctive *white* stripe on the flanks. Purple gallinule (*Porphyrula martinica*) is *metallic green-blue* and has a *pale blue* frontal shield and *orange-red* bill.
Status: Abundant resident and common migrant.

Family Charadriidae (Plovers)

(Total recorded: 9 species – Migrant 4 spp., Vagrant 5 spp.)

◆ 89. Semipalmated Plover

Charadrius semipalmatus

Length: 7 inches (18 cm)

Identification: A small, plump brown plover found singly, in pairs and small flocks. Associates with other shorebirds. White collar and throat, with a conspicuous white supercilium. Belly pure white with a single, thick brown breast band. Black bill and orange legs. *Breeding* birds have a single, thick black breast band and an orange bill with a black tip. Brown head has black and white patterning. Legs orange. Sexes alike. *In flight* has single white wing stripe and white edges to brown rump and tail.
Habitat: Ponds, mudflats, fields, agricultural land, golf courses, beaches and coasts.
Similar species: Wilson's Plover (*Charadrius wilsonia*) which has a *thick black* bill and *pink-grey* legs. In flight has *thin* white wing stripe and a rectangular brown tail with *thick* white edging. Piping Plover (*Charadrius melodus*) which is *smaller, pale grey* and has *conspicuous*

Semipalmated Plover

black forehead stripe. In flight has *white* rump and distinctive *black tip* to tail.

Status: Common migrant.

◆ **92. Killdeer**   *Charadrius vociferus*

Length: 10.5 inches (26 cm)

Identification: A medium-sized slender brown plover often found in small flocks. White collar and throat, with black and white patterning on a pale brown head. Belly pure white with distinctive twin black breast bands. Black eye with distinctive red border. Sexes alike. *In flight* has conspicuous pale golden rump and tail, white edging to the trailing edge of wing and a single white wing stripe. Tail long and pointed with a single black and white band at the tip.

Habitat: Fields, agricultural land, open areas, golf courses and ponds.

Similar species: The *larger* size, *golden rump* and *tail* and *double breast band* distinguish this species from all similar 'ringed' plovers.

Status: Common migrant.

Killdeer

◆ 94. American Lesser Golden Plover *Pluvialis dominica*

Length: 10.5 inches (26 cm)

Identification: A medium-sized, stocky brown plover often found in small flocks. Associates with other shorebirds. Back and crown chocolate brown, belly paler with fine, sparse streaking. Pale supercilium, black beak, eyes and legs. *Breeding* birds golden brown with black belly, throat and face. A conspicuous white line starts at the forehead and borders the back down to the breast. *In flight* has brown wings, rump and tail. Sexes similar.

Habitat: Mudflats, fields, open areas and golf courses.

Similar species: Black bellied Plover (*Pluvialis squatarola*) which is *larger* and has a *pale grey* back. In flight has *white* wing stripe, *white* rump and striped tail and conspicuous *black armpits* (axillae).

Status: Frequent migrant.

◆ **96. Black-bellied Plover**   *Pluvialis squatarola*

Length: 12 inches (31 cm)

Identification: A large, stocky, pale grey plover normally found in small flocks. Back and crown grey and mottled, belly paler. Pale supercilium, black beak, eyes and legs. *Breeding* birds have a black belly, throat and face with a conspicuous thick white line starting from forehead and bordering the back down to mid-belly. *In flight* has bold white wing stripe, white rump and white barred tail and conspicuous black 'armpits' (axillae). Sexes similar. *Immatures* similar to non-breeding birds, but are more golden brown with fine streaks on belly.
Habitat: Mudflats, fields, open areas, golf courses and coast.
Similar species: Lesser Golden Plover (*Pluvialis dominica*) which is smaller and has a *chocolate brown* back. In flight has *brown* rump and tail and *lacks* the white wing stripes and black axillae.
Status: Common migrant.

Family Scolopacidae (Snipes, Godwits, Sandpipers, Stints, etc.)

(Total recorded: 36 species – Migrant 15 spp., Pelagic 2 spp., Vagrant 19 spp.)

◆ **98. Common (Wilson's) Snipe** *Gallinago gallinago*

Length: 10.5 inches (27 cm)

Identification: A squat and secretive bird, normally only encountered when flushed from its hiding place. Upperparts patterned with brown and black, with several long white stripes on the back. Underparts tan and white, mottled with black and brown. Pale brown head striped with dark brown and a long dark yellow-green bill. Sexes alike. *In flight* erratic with brown, black and white wings, white back stripes and rufous banded tail.
Habitat: Swamps, ponds, mudflats and fields.
Similar species: Short-billed Dowitcher (*Limnodromus griseus*) has *longer* black bill and *lacks* white striping on back. In flight has *white wedge on back* and a *white, heavily barred tail*. American Woodcock (*Scolopax minor*) is *shorter* and more *squat*, with *rounded* wings, *rufous* underparts and *grey and brown* upperparts.
Status: Common migrant.

Whimbrel

◆ 100. Whimbrel   *Numenius phaeopus*

Length: 17.5 inches (45 cm)

Identification: A large brown wader with a prominent decurved bill. Found singly, in pairs or in small flocks. Upperparts pale brown with white flecks, underparts pale with finely streaked neck and breast. Conspicuous brown eye stripe and striped crown. Legs grey-blue. Sexes alike. *In flight* has brown wings, rump and tail (although European vagrants have a pale rump).

Habitat: Ponds, mudflats, fields, agricultural land, open areas, beaches, coast and offshore islands.

Similar species: The long, *strongly decurved* bill and *grey-blue* legs should prevent misidentification with other large shorebirds.

Status: Uncommon vagrant.

◆ 102. Spotted Sandpiper   *Actitis macularia*

Length: 7.5 inches (19 cm)

Identification: A small sandpiper that continuously tilts back and forth while feeding. Found singly, in pairs or in small flocks.

Spotted Sandpiper with winter plumage

Associates with other shorebirds. Brown back, light underparts with a 'smudge' near the shoulder that creates the appearance of a white wedge at the base of the wing. Head brown with distinctive white supercilium. Bill dark orange, legs yellow. *Breeding* birds are heavily spotted on the underparts. Bill and legs bright orange. *In flight* has a white wing stripe and a brown, lightly striped tail. Sexes alike.

Habitat: Ponds, mudflats, fields, agricultural land, golf courses, beaches and coast.

Similar species: Solitary Sandpiper (*Tringa solitaria*) which *lacks* the heavy spotting in breeding birds and has a white eye ring. In flight it *lacks* the white wing stripe and has a white tail *heavily barred* with thick black bars. The rare Wood Sandpiper (*Tringa glareola*) lacks the heavy spotting in breeding birds, has *yellow* legs and more *buffy* underparts. In flight it *lacks* the white wing stripe and has a *white* rump and *finely barred* white tail.

Status: Common migrant.

Solitary Sandpiper

◆ 103. Solitary Sandpiper   *Tringa solitaria*

Length: 8.5 inches (22 cm)

Identification: A small sandpiper found singly, in pairs or in small flocks. Associates with other shorebirds. Dark brown back spotted with white flecks, breast white with throat and chest heavily streaked with brown. Brown head with a conspicuous white eye ring. Bill black and legs greenish. Sexes alike. *In flight* has brown wings and a white tail crossed with heavy black bars.

Habitat: Ponds, mudflats, agricultural land and fields.

Similar species: Spotted Sandpiper (*Actitis macularia*), which is *smaller* with a *shorter* neck, *lacks* the white flecks on its back and in breeding plumage is *heavily spotted* on its underparts. In flight has a *brown* tail and *white* wing stripe. Lesser Yellowlegs (*Tringa flavipes*), which is *taller* and more *slender*, with *longer yellow* legs. In flight has *finely barred* white tail. The rare Wood Sandpiper (*Tringa glareola*) *lacks* the white eye ring and has *yellow* legs and more *buffy* underparts. In flight has a *white* rump and *finely barred* white tail.

Status: Common migrant.

◆ **106. Greater Yellowlegs**   *Tringa melanoleuca*

Length: 14 inches (35 cm)

Identification: A tall, slender, long-necked sandpiper found singly, in pairs and in small flocks. Associates with other shorebirds. Grey back and crown, flecked with white. Long black bill and pale grey base and long yellow legs. *Breeding* birds have darker brown back, flecked with white. Sexes alike. *In flight* has brown wings and back, white rump and a white, thinly barred tail. Faint white spotting on inner primaries.

Habitat: Ponds, mudflats, fields, agricultural land and golf courses.

Similar species: Most easily confused with Lesser Yellowlegs (*Tringa flavipes*) which is *smaller* with *shorter, all black* bill. In flight lacks white spotting on inner primaries. Willet (*Catoptrophorus semipalmatus*) is *larger* and more *heavily* built, with *pale grey* legs. In flight has *thick white* wing stripes with *black* trailing edges and shoulders. Common Greenshank (*Tringa nebularia*) is *smaller* with *greenish* legs. In flight has a distinctive *white wedge* extending up back.

Status: Frequent migrant.

◆ **107. Lesser Yellowlegs**   *Tringa flavipes*

Length: 10.5 inches (26 cm)

Identification: A tall slender, long-necked sandpiper found singly, in pairs and in small flocks. Associates with other shorebirds. Grey back and crown, heavily flecked with white. Underparts white, with sides flecked brown. Medium-sized black bill and long, yellow legs. *Breeding* birds have darker brown back, flecked with white. Sexes alike. *In flight* has brown wings and back, white rump and a white, thinly barred tail.

Habitat: Ponds, mudflats, fields, agricultural land and golf courses.

Similar species: Most easily confused with Greater Yellowlegs (*Tringa melanoleuca*) which is *larger* with *longer black* bill with a *pale grey base*. In flight has *faint white* spotting on inner primaries. Common Greenshank (*Tringa nebularia*) is *larger* with *greenish* legs. In flight has a distinctive *white wedge* extending up back. Solitary Sandpiper (*Tringa solitaria*) is *smaller* and more *stocky* with distinct *white eye ring*. Legs *shorter* and *greenish yellow*. In flight has *black* rump extending in *black line* through centre of tail with *thick black horizontal* striping. Stilt Sandpiper (*Calidris himantopus*) is smaller, has *yellow-green* legs and *lacks* side spotting.

Status: Common migrant

Greater Yellowlegs

Lesser Yellowlegs

109. Ruddy Turnstone   *Arenaria interpres*

Length: 9.5 inches (24 cm)

Identification: A small, chunky brown shorebird found singly, in pairs and in small flocks. Small grey bill and short yellow-orange legs. A large brown 'bib' extends on to the white chest. *Breeding* birds have a chestnut back and wings, flecked with black and white. The head has distinctive, bold black and white markings. Legs bright orange and bill black. Sexes alike. *In flight* has a complex, unique pattern of chestnut, black and white.
Habitat: Ponds, mudflats, fields, agricultural land, golf courses, docks, beaches and coast.
Similar species: Distinctive.
Status: Abundant migrant.

113. Pectoral Sandpiper   *Calidris melanotos*

Length: 8.5 inches (22 cm)

Identification: A medium-sized, plump sandpiper with a longish neck. Usually in small flocks, associating with other shorebirds. Brown upperparts mottled and lined with white flecks. Heavily streaked brown neck and breast ends with a clear demarcation with the white underparts. Pale supercilium. Legs and bill yellow-green. *Males* larger and darker than females. *In flight* has thin white wing stripe, a white-bordered black rump and a black and brown tail.
Habitat: Ponds, mudflats, fields, agricultural land and golf courses.
Similar species: The *clear demarcation* of breast streaking with white underparts and the green-yellow legs should prevent misidentification with 'peep' sandpipers.
Status: Common migrant.

116. Least Sandpiper   *Calidris minutilla*

Length: 6 inches (15 cm)

Identification: A small 'peep' sandpiper found in small flocks. Associates with other shorebirds. Pale brown back streaked with white. Short black bill and yellow-green legs. Underparts pale with fine brown streaking on throat and upper chest. Head brown with pale grey supercilium. *In flight* has thin white wing stripe and a brown tail half bordered by white. Sexes alike.

Ruddy Turnstone is winter plumage

Pectoral Sandpiper

Least Sandpiper

Habitat: Ponds, mudflats, fields, agricultural land, golf courses, beaches and coast.
Similar species: The *small* size and *yellow-green* legs should prevent misidentification with similar sized 'peeps'.
Status: Common migrant.

◆ **120. Stilt Sandpiper**   *Calidris himantopus*

Length: 8.5 inches (22 cm)

Identification: A medium sized, tall and slender sandpiper found singly, in pairs and in small flocks. Associates with other shorebirds. Pale brown-grey upperparts and white supercilium, long black, slightly decurved bill and long, yellow-green legs. *Breeding* birds have brown-grey upperparts mottled and edged with pale brown. Sexes alike. *In flight* they have white rump and finely barred tail.
Habitat: Ponds and mudflats.
Similar species: Lesser Yellowlegs (*Tringa flavipes*) is *larger* with *straighter* bill and *bright yellow* legs. Common Greenshank (*Tringa nebularia*) is larger with *greenish* legs. In flight has a distinctive *white wedge* extending up back. Solitary Sandpiper (*Tringa solitaria*) is *smaller* and more *stocky* with distinct *white eye ring*. In flight has

black rump extending in *black line* through centre of tail with *thick black horizontal* striping. Short-billed Dowitcher (*Limnodromus griseus*) and Long-billed Dowitcher (*Limnodromus scolopaceus*) *lack* the streaked and barred underparts of breeding birds, are *more stocky* and have a *longer* bill.

Status: Frequent migrant.

◆ 121. Semipalmated Sandpiper *Calidris pusilla*

Length: 5.5 inches (14 cm)

Identification: A small 'peep' sandpiper found in small flocks. Associates with other shorebirds. Pale grey-brown back streaked with brown. Short black bill and legs. Underparts pale with fine brown streaking on throat and upper chest. Head grey-brown with pale supercilium. *In flight* has thin white wing stripe and a brown tail half bordered by white. Sexes alike.

Habitat: Ponds, mudflats, fields, agricultural land, golf courses, beaches and coast.

Similar species: Most easily confused with very similar Western Sandpiper (*Calidris mauri*), which is *slightly larger* and has a *slight decurve* to the tip of the *thickly based* bill. Also more *heavily* streaked on the breast. Least Sandpiper (*Calidris minutilla*) which is *smaller*

Semipalmated Sandpiper

and has a more *heavily* streaked breast and *yellow-green* legs. Baird's Sandpiper (*Calidris bairdii*) which is *larger* and the wings *extend beyond the tip of the tail*. Breast is *buffy*. White-rumped Sandpiper (*Calidris mauri*) which is *larger* and the wings extend beyond the tip of the tail. Sides *streaked* and *spotted* and in flight has a *distinctive white* rump.
Status: Abundant migrant.

◆ 123. Sanderling   *Calidris alba*

Length: 8 inches (20 cm)

Identification: A small, plump pale grey shorebird found singly, in pairs or in small flocks. Pale grey back, wings, neck and crown with white underparts. Black bill and legs. *Breeding* birds have ruddy brown back, wings, head, neck and breast speckled with black. Sexes alike. *In flight* has white wing stripe bordered by black and a dark tail edged with white.
Habitat: Docks, beaches and coast.
Similar species: Could be confused with several 'peep' sandpipers (i.e. Baird's Sandpiper (*Calidris bairdii*) or White-rumped Sandpiper (*Calidris fuscicollis*), but pale grey, black and white body colours should prevent misidentification.
Status: Common migrant.

Sanderling showing summer plumage

◆ **124. Short-billed Dowitcher** *Limnodromus griseus*

Length: 11 inches (28 cm)

Identification: A medium-sized, stocky wader with a very long, black bill. Found singly, in pairs or in small flocks. Associates with other shorebirds. Grey upperparts and white underparts, lightly streaked on breast and sides. Bill black and legs greenish yellow. White supercilium. *Breeding* birds have brown upperparts flecked with white and black. Ruddy brown neck, breast and flanks. Belly white. Sexes alike. *In flight* has thin white wing stripe and trailing edges, a white wedge on the back and a white, heavily barred tail.

Habitat: Ponds, mudflats, fields, agricultural land and golf courses.

Similar species: Most easily confused with Long-billed Dowitcher (*Limnodromus scolopaceus*) which generally has a *longer* bill and, in breeding plumage, has *darker*, more *heavily barred* underparts with *little*, if any, white on the belly. Common Snipe (*Gallinago gallinago*) has a *shorter*, *dark yellow-green* bill and a *black striped* crown. Body is *heavily streaked* with *white* and *black*.

Status: Uncommon vagrant.

Short-billed Dowitcher

◆ **132. Wilson's Phalarope**   *Phalaropus tricolor*

Length: 9 inches (23 cm)

Identification: A solitary, medium-sized, slender phalarope. Pale grey upperparts and white underparts, with a thin black bill and green-yellow legs. Pale grey eye stripe that does not extend to bill, stopping just in front of eye. Sexes alike in winter plumage, but differ in breeding plumage. *Male breeding* birds have grey-brown upperparts and black stripes on the crown and through the eye that extend down the back of the neck. White throat. Cinnamon-pinkish wash to neck and breast. *Female breeding* birds have dark grey upperparts streaked with maroon. Thick black eye stripe continues down back of neck, becoming red-maroon and curving across back. Neck and breast have a cinnamon-pink wash. *In flight* have white rump and tail.

Habitat: Ponds and fields.

Similar species: All other phalaropes have a *white* wing stripe and *grey* tail in flight. Breeding birds have distinctively different colour patterns. Winter plumage of Red-necked Phalarope (*Phalaropus lobatus*) has *black crown* and *conspicuous black* eye stripe. Winter plumage of Red Phalarope (*Phalaropus fulicaria*) has *white forehead*, *dark grey* crown patch and *dark grey* eye stripe.

Status: Occasional vagrant.

Family Laridae (Jaegers, Skuas, Gulls, Terns and Skimmers)

(Total recorded: 34 species – Resident 1 sp., Migrant 2 spp., Pelagic 4 spp., Vagrant 27 spp.)

◆ **133. Great Skua**   *Catharacta skua*

Length: 23 inches (58 cm)

Identification: A large, stocky gull-like bird with eagle-like, broad wings. Body chocolate brown with paler mottling and streaking, with darker brown primaries and tail feathers. Conspicuous white wing patches. Sexes alike.

Habitat: Aerial and offshore, occasionally coast.

Similar species: South Polar Skua (*Catharacta maccormicki*) is uniform *grey-brown* and *lacks* mottling and streaking. Could be confused with immature jaegers, but all *lack* white wing patches.
Status: Frequent pelagic migrant.

◆ **135. Pomarine Jaeger**   *Stercorarius pomarinus*

Length: 21 inches (53 cm)

Identification: A slender, fast moving jaeger with two colour phases. *Dark phase* birds are all dark brown, with lighter brown primaries. *Light phase* birds have dark brown back, wings and tail, with a black capped head. Cheeks are pale yellow, throat and belly white with a pale brown collar. Both phases have broad, twisted central tail feathers extending from main tail. Sexes alike. *Immature* birds are heavily barred and mottled brown.
Habitat: Aerial and offshore, rarely coast.
Similar species: Parasitic Jaeger (*Stercorarius parasiticus*) is smaller and has *small, pointed* central tail feathers. Long-tailed Jaeger (*Stercorarius longicaudus*) *lacks* the brown collar and has *very long, pointed* central tail feathers. Immatures could be confused with Great Skua (*Catharacta skua*) which has distinct *white wing patches*.
Status: Frequent pelagic migrant.

◆ **136. Parasitic Jaeger**   *Stercorarius parasiticus*

Length: 18 inches (45 cm)

Identification: A small, slender jaeger with two colour phases. *Dark phase* birds are all dark brown with lighter brown primaries. Light phase birds have dark brown back, wings and tail, with a black capped head. Cheeks are pale yellow, throat and belly white with a pale brown collar and pale brown vent. Both phases have short, pointed central tail fathers extending from main tail. Sexes alike. *Immature* birds are heavily barred and mottled brown and white.
Habitat: Aerial and offshore, rarely coast.
Similar species: Pomarine Jaeger (*Stercorarius pomarinus*) is *larger* and has *broad, twisted* central tail feathers. Long-tailed Jaeger (*Stercorarius longicaudus*) *lacks* the brown collar and has *very long, pointed* central tail feathers. Immatures could be confused with Great Skua (*Catharacta skua*) which has distinct *white wing patches*.
Status: Frequent pelagic migrant.

◆ 140. Great Black-backed Gull   *Larus marinus*

Length: 30 inches (76 cm)

Identification: A very large gull with black back and wings. Head, neck, tail and underparts white. Trailing edge and shoulders of leading edge white. Thick yellow bill with bright red patch on lower mandible. Eyes yellow and legs pink. Sexes alike. Immatures mottled brown and white. Primaries darker brown. Bill and eyes black, legs pinkish grey.

Habitat: Coast, docks, bays and inlets.

Similar species: Immatures could be confused with the immatures of other gulls, but it is *larger* and has a *mottled white* rump. Adults could be confused with Lesser Black-backed Gull (*Larus fuscus*) which is *smaller* and has a *paler back* and *yellow* legs.

Status: Frequent vagrant.

◆ 141. Lesser Black-backed Gull   *Larus fuscus*

Length: 21 inches (56 cm)

Identification: A large gull with a slaty grey back, mottled pale brown head and white breast. The bill is bright yellow with a conspicuous red spot at the tip of the lower mandible. Legs are yellow. *Breeding adults* have a pure white head. *In flight* has thin white edge to leading and trailing edges of wings. Primaries are broadly tipped black, with leading edge primaries fully black and displaying a single prominent white spot. *Juveniles* have pink legs and black beak and are mottled pale brown.

Habitat: Coastal, offshore islands, ponds and docks.

Similar species: Glaucous Gull has a *very pale* grey back with *no black* on wings. Herring Gull is somewhat *larger* and has a *paler grey* back. Juveniles are a *darker grey-brown*.

Status: Occasional vagrant.

◆ 142. Herring Gull   *Larus argentatus*

Length: 25 inches (64 cm)

Identification: A large gull with pale grey upperparts. Head, neck, tail and underparts white. Black and white tipped primaries and trailing edge and shoulders of leading edge white. Bill yellow with bright red patch on lower mandible. Eyes yellow and legs pink. Sexes alike.

Herring Gull in first winter plumage

Immatures chocolate brown, mottled with darker brown. Primaries darker brown and rump brown. Bill and eyes black, legs pink.
Habitat: Coast, docks, bays and inlets.
Similar species: Ring-billed Gull (*Larus delawarensis*); adults are *smaller*, have a *black ring* on bill and *yellow* legs. Immatures are *smaller*, paler, have a *white* rump and have *pinkish grey* legs.
Status: Frequent vagrant.

◆ 143. Ring-billed Gull   *Larus delawarensis*

Length: 19 inches (48 cm)

Identification: A medium-sized gull with pale grey upperparts. Head, neck, tail and underparts white. Black and white tipped primaries and trailing edge white. Bill yellow with black ring. Eyes and legs yellow. Sexes alike. *Immatures* pale brown, mottled with darker brown. Primaries darker brown. Bill and eyes black, legs pinkish grey.
Habitat: Coast, docks, bays and inlets.
Similar species: No other similarly sized gull has a black ring on a yellow bill. Immature Herring Gull (*Larus argentatus*) is *larger, darker* and has *pink legs*.
Status: Common vagrant.

Ring-billed Gull in winter plumage

◆ 147. Bonaparte's Gull   *Larus philadelphia*

Length: 13.5 inches (34 cm)

Identification: A small, pale grey backed gull with black beak and red feet. Sexes alike. *Breeding adults* have a black head, which is reduced to a small black smudge behind the eye in the winter. Wings have a broad strip of white on the leading edge, broadening towards the tip. Primaries are thickly tipped with black. *Juveniles* have pink legs and the wings are speckled with dark grey.

Habitat: Coastal, shoreline, offshore islands, ponds and docks.

Similar species: Franklin's Gull is *darker* grey, with a *partial white eye-ring* in breeding plumage and darker grey wings *lacking* the white streak on the leading edge. Common Black-headed Gull is *larger* and has a *red* bill. Laughing Gull is *larger*, is *slate grey*, has a *partial white eye ring* in breeding plumage and has *broadly black tipped* wings.

Status: Occasional vagrant.

◆ 149. Black-legged Kittiwake   *Rissa tridactyla*

Length: 17 inches (43 cm)

Identification: A small, slender gull with pale grey back and wings. Head, neck, tail and underparts white. Wings have conspicuous black tips. Eyes dark red, bill yellow and legs black. Sexes alike. *Immatures* have distinctive black 'M-shaped' marking extending across wings and back. Tail has black tip and bill is black.

Habitat: Aerial and offshore, occasionally coast and beaches.

Similar species: The *small* size and combination of *yellow* bill and *black* legs should prevent misidentification with similar gull species.

Status: Frequent vagrant.

◆ 151. Gull-billed Tern   *Sterna nilotica*

Length: 14 inches (36 cm)

Identification: A medium-sized tern with a shallow forked tail. Upperparts pale grey, underparts white. Head has smudged, grey cap and nape. Thick, black bill and black legs. Sexes alike. *Breeding* birds have a black cap that continues down the nape. *Immatures* are similar to non-breeding adults, although back is more mottled.

Habitat: Aerial and offshore, occasionally in harbours and over offshore islands.

Similar species: The combination of *thick, black* bill and *black* legs should prevent misidentification with other terns.

Status: Uncommon vagrant.

◆ 153. Common Tern   *Sterna hirundo*

Length: 14.5 inches (37 cm)

Identification: A small, sleek tern with a deeply forked tail. Upperparts pale grey, underparts white. White forehead with dark grey nape patch extending into eye stripe. Bill dark grey with reddish base, legs dark. Primaries darker grey with white on trailing edge and on shoulders of leading edge. Primaries on underwing are pale grey, with a white wedge on the primaries near the base of the wing. Sexes alike. *Breeding* birds have a black cap that continues down the nape, a bright red bill with a black tip and bright red legs. *Immatures* are similar to non-breeding adults, although back is more mottled.

Habitat: Aerial, in harbours and over offshore islands.

Similar species: Easily confused with Arctic Tern (*Sterna paradisaea*), which in breeding birds *lacks* the *black* tip to the red bill, has a *greyish* belly and *white* cheeks. Non-breeding birds are very similar, but have a *longer, more deeply forked tail* and *white* primaries on the underwing. Forster's Tern (*Sterna forsteri*) which has an *orange* bill and has *pale* grey primaries and a *pale grey* forked tail. Non-breeding birds have a distinctive *dark grey eye stripe*. Roseate Tern (*Sterna dougallii*). Breeding birds have a *black* bill and a *pale grey* wash to belly. Non-breeding birds are similar but have a *longer* forked tail, *lack* the red base to the bill and have a more *diffuse* nape patch.

Status: Common resident (in breeding season: April to November) and migrant.

◆ 154. Arctic Tern   *Sterna paradisaea*

Length: 15.5 inches (39 cm)

Identification: A small, sleek tern with a deeply forked tail. Upperparts pale grey, underparts white. White forehead with dark grey nape patch extending into eye stripe. Bill dark grey with reddish base, legs dark. Primaries darker grey with white on trailing edge and on shoulders of leading edge. Primaries on underwing are white. Sexes alike. *Breeding* birds have a black cap that continues down the nape, a bright red bill and bright red legs. Belly is pale grey and the cheeks are white. *Immatures* are similar to non-breeding adults, although back is more mottled.

Habitat: Aerial, mainly offshore although occasionally in harbours and over offshore islands.

Similar species: Easily confused with Common Tern (*Sterna hirundo*), which in breeding birds has a *black* tip to the red bill and a *white* belly. Non-breeding birds are very similar, but have a *shorter, more shallowly forked* tail and *pale grey* primaries on the underwing, with a *white* wedge on the primaries at the base of the wings. Forster's Tern (*Sterna forsteri*), which has an *orange* bill and has *pale* grey primaries and a *pale grey* forked tail. Non-breeding birds have a distinctive *dark grey eye stripe*. Roseate Tern (*Sterna dougallii*); breeding birds have a *black* bill and *pale grey* wash to belly. Non-breeding birds are similar but have a *longer* forked tail, *lack* the red base to the bill and have a more *diffuse* nape patch.

Status: Common pelagic migrant.

◆ 156. Sooty Tern   *Sterna fuscata*

Length: 16 inches (41 cm)

Identification: A large tern with a black back, wings and tail. Underparts and outer tail feathers white, inner tail feathers black. Underparts of tail and underwing white. White forehead, with a black cap and eye stripe, extending into black back. Black bill and legs. Sexes alike. *Immatures* have dark grey head, back, wings, tail and belly. Lower belly and vent white. Back and wings flecked with white.

Habitat: Aerial, mainly offshore.

Similar species: Bridled Tern (*Sterna anaethetus*), which is *smaller*, has a *white collar* and more extensive white on tail feathers. Brown Noddy (*Anous stolidus*) resembles immatures, but is *completely brown*, save for a *pale* crown.

Status: Uncommon vagrant and possibly an extirpated breeding resident.

Sooty Tern

◆ 157. Least Tern   *Sterna antillarum*

Length: 9 inches (23 cm)

Identification: A very small tern with a deeply forked tail. Upperparts pale grey, underparts white. White forehead with dark grey nape and eye stripe. Bill and legs black. Primaries darker grey with white on trailing edge and on shoulders of leading edge. Leading edge of first primaries black. Sexes alike. *Breeding* birds have a white forehead and a black cap that continues down the nape, a yellow bill with a black tip and yellow legs. *Immatures* are pale mottled buff and white with a distinct black eye stripe.

Habitat: Aerial, mainly offshore islands, coastal, harbours and beaches.

Similar species: The *small* size, *yellow* bill and *white* forehead should prevent misidentification with other terns.

Status: Uncommon vagrant.

Least Tern

163. Black Tern   *Chilidonias niger*

Length: 9.5 inches (24 cm)

Identification: A small, pale grey tern with shallow forked tail. Upperparts pale grey, underparts white with a distinct grey smudge creating a half-collar, from the wings down. Dark grey cap and cheek patch. Bill black and legs dark red. *Breeding* birds are very distinctive, being black with dark grey wings and tail. Head, neck and belly black. Undertail coverts white. Sexes alike. *Immatures* similar to non-breeding adults, with more barring above.
Habitat: Aerial, over coast, ponds and lakes.
Similar species: Distinctive.
Status: Occasional vagrant.

Family Pandionidae (Osprey)

(Total recorded: 1 species – Migrant 1 sp.)

169. Osprey   *Pandion haliaetus*

Length: 23 inches (60 cm)

Identification: A large, slender, fish-eating raptor. Brown above with white breast, belly and legs. Head with small crest and prominent eye stripe. Yellow eye and pale grey bill. *Females* identical to males, except for a scattering of brown feathers in a necklace across the breast. *In flight*, dark brown shoulder patches, barred brown and white flight feathers and a barred brown and white tail become apparent.
Habitat: Aerial, over lakes and coastal areas.
Similar species: Distinctive.
Status: Frequent migrant.

Family Accipitridae (Kites, Eagles and Hawks)

(Total recorded: 9 species – Vagrant 9 spp.)

◆ 171. Swallow-tailed Kite   *Elanoides forficatus*

Length: 23 inches (60 cm)

Identification: A very distinctive raptor. White head, breast and belly with black primaries and secondaries and black tail feathers. *In flight* it has a long, deeply forked tail and slender, graceful wings. Sexes alike.
Habitat: Aerial, over open woodlands, ponds and marshes.
Similar species: Distinctive.
Status: Occasional vagrant.

◆ 173. Sharp-shinned Hawk   *Accipiter striatus*

Length: 14 inches (35 cm)

Identification: A small, typically hawk-shaped raptor with rounded wings and long tail. Dark grey above with a heavily red-brown streaked breast. Red eye, small yellow beak and yellow legs. *In flight* shows heavily barred wings and banded tail. *Immatures* are mottled brown and white above, with white breast mottled and streaked with red-brown markings. Eyes yellow. Sexes alike, although female is larger.
Habitat: Aerial, over woodlands, fields and coast.
Similar species: Cooper's Hawk (*Accipiter cooperii*), which is *larger* with a more *distinctive crown* and, in flight, a *rounded*, barred tail. Immatures have a more *finely* streaked breast with markings *fading* near belly. Northern Goshawk (*Accipiter gentilis*), which is *larger* with *conspicuous white eyebrow* and *finely* barred *pale* breast. *Immatures* are larger with *conspicuous white eyebrow* and *wavy* brown barring on tail.
Status: Occasional vagrant.

Family Falconidae (Falcons and Kestrels)

(Total recorded: 5 species – Migrant 1 sp., Vagrant 4 spp.)

◆ **180. Peregrine Falcon**   *Falco peregrinus*

Length: 20 inches (50 cm)

Identification: A large, powerfully built falcon. Dark grey back, wings and tail with a black cap and prominent black cheeks. Breast is pale brown with light spotting turning into heavy barring on belly. Long tail is heavily banded. *Immatures* are dark brown above with a heavily streaked breast.

Habitat: Aerial, over woodlands, agricultural land, open areas, coast and marshes.

Similar species: Merlin (*Falco columbarius*) which is *much smaller* and *lacks* the prominent black cheek markings.

Status: Occasional migrant.

Peregrine Falcon, immature (tame)

◆ 182. Merlin *Falco columbarius*

Length: 12 inches (31 cm)

Identification: A small falcon that resembles a miniature Peregrine Falcon. *Males* have a slate grey back, crown, wings and tail with a pale brown, streaked breast. Tail shows several thick dark bars, with the last band being much thicker. Conspicuous eyebrow and single vertical facial stripe. *Females* have a chocolate brown back, crown, wings and tail. Breast pale brown and heavily streaked. *Immatures* similar to females.

Habitat: Aerial, over woodlands, golf courses, open areas, agricultural land and fields.

Similar species: American Kestrel (*Falco sparverius*): males have *distinctive* black and white facial markings and a *rufous*, not grey, back; females have *distinctive* black and white facial markings and a *rufous* back and tail. Peregrine Falcon (*Falco peregrinus*) which is *larger* and has *prominent black* cheek markings.

Status: Common vagrant.

Merlin ♀

◆ 184. American Kestrel   *Falco sparverius*

Length: 10.5 inches (27 cm)

Identification: A small falcon which often hovers in the air for its prey. *Males* have a rufous back and black-tipped tail, grey and black wings. The head has a pale grey cap and two prominent vertical black stripes on white cheeks. Crown is rufous coloured and rufous undertail has single thick black, white-tipped, band. *Females* have brown, heavily barred wings, back and tail. Head paler than males and undertail heavily barred. *Immatures* are similar to adults, but are paler and more heavily barred.

Habitat: Aerial over woodlands, urban areas, golf courses, open areas, agricultural land and fields.

Similar species: Merlin (*Falco columbarius*): males are *larger* with an *all grey* back and *lack* the prominent facial markings; females are *larger* with *chocolate brown* back and tail and *lack* the prominent facial markings. Eurasian Kestrel (*Falco tinnunculus*) has a *pale grey* head and tail and a *single* vertical facial stripe.

Status: Frequent vagrant.

American Kestrel

Family Columbidae (Pigeons and Doves)

(Total recorded: 3 species – Resident 2 spp., Introduced 1 sp.)

◆ 185. Rock Dove (Feral Pigeon)   *Columba livia*

Length: 13 inches (33 cm)

Identification: A highly variable pigeon, typically in large flocks. The typical form has pale grey back, wings and tail. Black vertical stripe across border of wing coverts and secondaries and black trailing edge to secondaries. Pale grey rump. Pale grey head with white lore, irridescent neck, collar and upper breast. Sexes alike. It should be noted that there is an infinite variety of colours due to human breeding, ranging from all white individuals, through to browns, blacks and mottled effects.

Habitat: Urban sprawl, cliffs, fields, agricultural land.

Similar species: Distinctive.

Status: Introduced, abundant resident; considered a pest species.

◆ 186. Mourning Dove   *Zenaida macroura*

Length: 12 inches (31 cm)

Identification: A medium-sized, slender, long-tailed dove. Normally found in pairs. Pale brown upperparts, with dark brown flecks on wings. Crown pale grey, with black spot on cheek. Irridescence on side of neck. Rosy brown throat and belly. Elongate diamond-shaped tail brown with black and white edging. *Immatures* similar to adults, but are more heavily scaled and spotted and lack irridescence and rosy wash.

Habitat: Woodlands, agricultural land, open areas, marshes, coast and fields.

Similar species: The only other dove species on the island, the Common Ground Dove (*Columbina passerina*), is much *smaller*, with *rufous* primary feathers and a *short, stubby* tail.

Status: Abundant resident and migrant.

Mourning Dove

◆ **187. Common Ground-Dove** *Columbina passerina*

Length: 6.5 inches (17 cm)

Identification: A diminutive, plump dove with pale brown upperparts and pinkish underparts. Normally found in pairs. Primaries are rufous, with black tips. Crown pale grey and eyes red. Brown spotting on wings. *Females* similar to males, but lack the grey crown and are somewhat paler.

Habitat: Woodland, agricultural land, open areas, marshes, fields and coast.

Similar species: The only other dove species on the island, the Mourning Dove (*Zenaida macroura*) is much *larger*, with *pale* grey wings and a *long, diamond-shaped* tail.

Status: Common resident.

Common Ground-Dove

Family Cuculidae (Cuckoos and Coucals)

(Total recorded: 2 species – Vagrant 2 spp.)

◆ **188. Yellow-billed Cuckoo** *Coccyzus americanus*

Length: 12 inches (31 cm)

Identification: A slender, skulking cuckoo with chocolate brown upperparts and white underparts. Uppertail brown with black and white edging, undertail dark with large white spots. Bill yellow, although upper mandible darker. Yellow eye ring. Rufous, black tipped primaries. Sexes alike.

Habitat: Woodland, gardens, agricultural land and fields.

Similar species: Black-billed Cuckoo (*Coccyzus erythropthalmus*), which has a *black* bill, *red* eye ring, brown tail edged with *dark brown* and white, and *lacks* the white spots on the undertail.

Status: Frequent vagrant.

Yellow-billed Cuckoo

Family Tytonidae (Barn and Grass Owls)

(Total recorded: 1 species – Resident 1 spp.)

◆ 190. Barn Owl   *Tyto alba*

Length: 16 inches (41 cm)

Identification: A pale, ghostly owl with a distinctive white, heart-shaped facial disc. Upperparts pale brown flecked with pale grey, underparts white with sparse black spotting. White facial disc bordered with brown. Sexes alike.

Habitat: Woodland, cliffs, agricultural land, grasslands and fields.

Similar species: Distinctive.

Status: Frequent resident.

Barn Owl

Family Strigidae (True Owls)

(Total recorded: 8 species – Vagrant 8 spp.)

◆ **192. Short-eared Owl**   *Asio flammeus*

Length: 15 inches (38 cm)

Identification: A medium-sized owl with heavily mottled brown and white upperparts. Breast buff and heavily streaked with a dark brown, fading into a white belly faintly streaked with brown. Pale facial disc has a thin white and black border. Eyes sulphur yellow.

Short 'ear' tufts. *In flight* has distinctive black wrist patches and wing tips. Sexes alike.

Habitat: Woodland, agricultural land, grasslands and fields.

Similar species: Long-eared Owl (*Asio otus*) has *rufous* cheeks and *long, conspicuous* 'ear' tufts. Barred Owl (*Strix varia*) *lacks* the 'ear' tufts and has a *barred* facial disc.

Status: Occasional vagrant.

◆ **197. Northern Saw-whet Owl**   *Aegolius acadicus*
Length: 8 inches (20 cm)

Identification: A small, stumpy owl. Upperparts brown flecked with white, underparts white with rufous brown streaks. Forehead heavily flecked with white. Distinctive white eyebrows and facial area. Eyes sulphur yellow. Sexes alike. *Immatures* have dark brown upperparts and rufous brown underparts, with a distinct white 'V' on the forehead.

Habitat: Woodlands.

Similar species: Distinctive.

Status: Uncommon vagrant.

Family Caprimulgidae (Nightjars)

(Total recorded: 3 species – Vagrant 3 spp.)

◆ **200. Common Nighthawk**   *Chordeiles minor*
Length: 9.5 inches (24 cm)

Identification: A small, hawk-like, nocturnal bird. Upperparts mottled brown, grey and white, underparts buff and heavily barred. *Males* have a distinctive white chin, white tail band and wing bars. *Females* similar to males but have buff chin and lack white tail band.

Habitat: Woodland, agricultural land, ponds, fields and golf courses.

Similar species: Visually almost identical to the Antillean Nighthawk (*Chordeiles gundlachii*), which is slightly smaller and more buffy below. Lesser Nighthawk (*Chordeiles acutipennis*) is *smaller, paler* and white wing bar is *closer* to the wing tip. In females, the wing bar is *buff*. Whip-poor-will (*Caprimulgus vociferus*) has a *black* chin, *white* half collar and *lacks* the white wing bar.

Status: Frequent vagrant.

Antillean Nighthawk (visually identical to Common Nighthawk)

Family Apodidae (Swifts)

(Total recorded: 3 species – Vagrant 3 spp.)

◆ **202. Chimney Swift**   *Chaetura pelagica*

Length: 5.5 inches (14 cm)

Identification: A long, scimitar-winged swift with an elongate, cigar-shaped body. Body chocolate brown with paler chin and breast. Tail short and squared. Sexes alike.

Habitat: Aerial, over fields, agricultural land, golf courses and ponds.

Similar species: Black Swift (*Cypseloides niger*) is *larger, black* and *lacks* the pale chin and breast. European Swift (*Apus apus*) is *black*, has a distinct *white* chin and a *forked* tail.
Status: Occasional vagrant.

Family Trochilidae (Hummingbirds)

(Total recorded: 1 species – Vagrant 1 sp.)

◆ 205. Ruby-throated Hummingbird   *Archilochus colubris*

Length: 3.5 inches (8.5 cm)

Identification: A very small irridescent green hummingbird. *Males* have a bright ruby-red throat and an olive green 'waistcoat'. *Females* have a white throat and belly.
Habitat: Gardens and fields.
Similar species: Distinctive.
Status: Uncommon vagrant.

Family Alcedinidae (Kingfishers)

(Total recorded: 1 species – Migrant 1 sp.)

◆ 206. Belted Kingfisher   *Ceryle alcyon*

Length: 13 inches (33 cm)

Identification: A large, heavily built kingfisher that often hovers before diving on its prey. *Males* have a slaty blue crest (looking like unkempt hair), slaty blue back, wings and tail. Head has a small white spot in front of the eye. Thick bill is black. Primaries are black and white. One slaty blue 'belt' extends across the breast. A second, rufous 'belt' extends across the belly and flanks. Belly, vent and undertail white. *Females* are the same as males, but lack the second rufous 'belt'.
Habitat: Ponds, coast and fields.
Similar species: Distinctive.
Status: Frequent migrant.

Belted Kingfisher ♀

Family Picidae (Woodpeckers)

(Total recorded: 4 species – Vagrant 4 spp.)

◆ 209. Yellow-bellied Sapsucker *Sphyrapicus varius*

Length: 8.5 inches (22 cm)

Identification: A medium-sized, black and white woodpecker. *Males* have a bright red forehead and throat patch, surrounded by black and white facial markings. Belly is pale yellow, fading to white at vent, and is lightly flecked on the flanks with pale brown. There is a distinctive large white wing patch that can be clearly seen in flight. *Females* are similar to males, but lack the bright red throat patch.

Habitat: Woodlands and mangroves.

Similar species: Downy Woodpecker (*Picoides pubescens*) has a bright red nape patch, lacks the bright red forehead and throat and has a white belly. It lacks the large white wing patch and has a white back.

Status: Occasional vagrant.

◆ **210. Downy Woodpecker**   *Picoides pubescens*

Length: 6.5 inches (16 cm)

Identification: A small, black and white woodpecker. *Males* have a black and white striped face and a small, bright red nape patch, white back, black wings spotted with white and a black tail with white outer tail feathers. *Female* similar to male but lacks the red nape patch.
Habitat: Woodlands.
Similar species: Yellow-bellied Sapsucker (*Sphyrapicus varius*) has a *yellowish* belly, bright red *forehead* and *lacks* the bright red nape patch.
Status: Uncommon vagrant.

Family Tyrannidae (Tyrant Flycatchers)

(Total recorded: 17 species – Introduced 1 sp., Vagrant 16 spp.)

◆ **211. Eastern Kingbird**   *Tyrannus tyrannus*

Length: 8.5 inches (22 cm)

Identification: A large dark grey and white tyrant flycatcher. Upper parts slaty grey, underparts pale grey and white. Head and cheeks black. Tail black, edged with white. Sexes alike.
Habitat: Woodlands, agricultural land and fields.
Similar species: Gray Kingbird (*Tyrannus dominicensis*) which has a *grey* head with a *darker grey* 'mask' and *pale yellow* wash to the lower belly.
Status: Occasional vagrant.

◆ **216. Greater Kiskadee**   *Pitangus sulphuratus*

Length: 9.5 inches (24 cm)

Identification: An unmistakable large tyrant flycatcher with a strident 'kis-ka-dee' call. Back brown with rufous brown wings. Underparts sulphur yellow. Head white with thick black eye stripe and a second black stripe below the crown. Crown sulphur yellow. Sexes alike.
Habitat: Woodlands, agricultural land, fields, ponds, mangroves, coast and offshore islands.
Similar species: Distinctive.
Status: Introduced, abundant resident; considered a pest species.

Greater Kiskadee

Greater Kiskadee fledgelings

◆ 217. Great Crested Flycatcher *Myiarchus crinitus*

Length: 8 inches (20 cm)

Identification: A large stocky flycatcher with dark brown back and wings. Crested head dark brown and throat and breast pale grey. Belly and vent sulphur yellow. Long, thick tail rufous brown. Sexes alike.
Habitat: Agricultural land, fields, gardens and golf courses.
Similar species: Western Kingbird (*Tyrannus verticalis*) *lacks* crest and has a *pale grey* head and *olive yellow* back. Tropical Kingbird (*Tyrannus melancholicus*) *lacks* crest and has a *pale grey* head, *darker grey face mask* and *olive yellow* back.
Status: Occasional vagrant.

◆ 219. Eastern Wood-Peewee *Contopus virens*

Length: 6.5 inches (16 cm)

Identification: A small, olive grey flycatcher. Upperparts olive grey, underparts pale grey with paler chin and vent. Wings dark grey with two white wing bars. Eye black, bill thin with black upper mandible and orange lower mandible. Legs black. Sexes alike.
Habitat: Agricultural land, fields, woodland and gardens.
Similar species: Eastern Phoebe (*Sayornis phoebe*) has pale *yellow wash* to lower belly and *lacks* the wing bars. Differs from all *Empidonax* flycatchers (Least, Acadian, Willow and Alder) by being *larger* and *lacking* the white eye ring and pale yellow wash to lower belly.
Status: Occasional vagrant.

◆ 225. Willow Flycatcher *Empidonax traillii*

Length: 5.5 inches (14 cm)

Identification: A slender, olive backed flycatcher. Head is pale grey, with a white throat and smudged grey breast. Back, wings and tail are olive brown, with two prominent white wing bars. Breast and flanks are white washed with pale yellow. Sexes alike.
Habitat: Agricultural land, gardens and parks.
Similar species: Virtually indistinguishable from Alder Flycatcher (indeed until recently these two species were considered to be a single species – Traill's Flycatcher), which has a *faint eye ring*, *slightly greener* back and a slightly *shorter* bill. The combination of two white wing bars and no eye ring should help to distinguish this

species from other similarly coloured flycatchers (such as Peewees for example).
Status: Uncommon vagrant.

Family Alaudidae (Larks)

(Total recorded: 2 species – Vagrant 2 spp.)

◆ 229. Horned Lark   *Eremophila alpestris*
Length: 7.5 inches (19 cm)

Identification: A plump, stocky brown lark often found in small flocks. Upperparts chocolate brown mottled with dark brown and black. Underparts pale buff and very lightly streaked on the flanks and upper breast. Black half collar extending across breast. Face and throat pale yellow, with distinctive black facial markings and two small black feathers that give the appearance of 'horns'. Sexes alike.
Habitat: Agricultural land, fields, golf courses and grassland.
Similar species: Distinctive.
Status: Frequent vagrant.

Family Hirundinidae (Swallows and Martins)

(Total recorded: 8 species – Migrant 3 spp., Vagrant 5 spp.)

◆ 230. Tree Swallow   *Tachycineta bicolor*
Length: 5.5 inches (14 cm)

Identification: A small swallow with glossy blue-black upperparts and clean white underparts. Tail slightly forked. *Females* slightly duller than males. *Immatures* have chocolate brown upperparts.
Habitat: Agricultural land, fields, grasslands and golf courses.
Similar species: Adults distinctive. Immatures could be confused with (i) Bank Swallow (*Riparia riparia*) which has a distinctive *brown breast-band* and (ii) Northern Rough-winged Swallow (*Stelgidopteryx serripennis*) which has a *brown* throat and upper breast.
Status: Occasional migrant.

◆ **231. Purple Martin**   *Progne subis*

Length: 8 inches (20 cm)

Identification: A large, unmistakable, glossy blue-black martin. Tail slightly forked. *Females* are similar to males, but have a white belly and mottled grey-blue throat and breast. *Immatures* are similar to females, but are duller.
Habitat: Agricultural land, fields, grasslands and golf courses.
Similar species: Distinctive.
Status: Frequent migrant.

◆ **233. Bank Swallow**   *Riparia riparia*

Length: 5.5 inches (14 cm)

Identification: A small brown and white swallow with a shallow forked tail. Head, back, wings and tail dark brown with a single brown breast band. Sexes alike. *Juveniles* similar to adults but have a more mottled appearance to the head.
Habitat: Agricultural land, clearings and over ponds.
Similar species: Could be confused with both Northern Rough-winged Swallow and juvenile Tree Swallow, but both species *lack* the brown breast band.
Status: Occasional vagrant.

◆ **234. Barn Swallow**   *Hirundo rustica*

Length: 7 inches (18 cm)

Identification: A medium-sized swallow with a deeply forked tail. Upperparts glossy blue-black, underparts buffy. Forehead and throat rufous. Tail has small white 'windows' visible in flight. *Females* and *immatures* similar to male, but paler.
Habitat: Agricultural land, fields, grasslands and golf courses.
Similar species: Cliff Swallow (*Hirundo pyrrhonota*) is *smaller*, has a *square* tail, *white* belly and a *pale buff* forehead and rump.
Status: Common migrant.

Barn Swallow

◆ 236. Cliff Swallow — *Hirundo pyrrhonota*

Length: 5.5 inches (14 cm)

Identification: A small swallow with dark blue back, wings, head and tail. Rump buffy brown and belly white. Frontal patch on head off white and sides of head and throat reddish. Black spotted vent and square tail. Sexes alike. *Juveniles* similar to adult but have a dark brown head.

Habitat: Agricultural land, clearings and over ponds.

Similar species: Very similar to rare Cave Swallow, which *lacks* the whitish forehead and has a *pale buff* throat. Barn Swallows have a *long forked* tail and a *dark blue* rump.

Status: Occasional vagrant.

Family Corvidae (Crows and Jays)

(Total recorded: 2 species – Introduced 1 sp., Vagrant 1 sp.)

◆ **239. Common (American) Crow**   *Corvus brachyrhynchos*

Length: 17.5 inches (45 cm)

Identification: An intelligent, large, unmistakable, black bird. Black eyes, thick black beak and black legs. Tail long and fan shaped. Sexes alike.
Habitat: Urban, agricultural land, fields, grasslands, golf courses, coast, cliffs, offshore islands and woodlands.
Similar species: Distinctive.
Status: Introduced, common resident, considered a pest species.

Family Muscicapidae (Thrushes)

(Total recorded: 13 species – Resident 1 sp., Migrant 2 spp., Vagrant 10 spp.)

◆ **248. Eastern Bluebird**   *Sialia sialis*

Length: 7 inches (18 cm)

Identification: A small, cobalt blue bird with rufous throat and breast. Belly and vent pale buff to white. *Males* have cobalt blue head, back, wings and tail. *Females* have a grey-brown head and back with cobalt blue edged wings. *Immatures* similar to female but have a brown breast heavily scaled with white and have white flecks on the wings.
Habitat: Agricultural land, fields and golf courses (where they commonly nest).
Similar species: Blue Grosbeak (*Guiraca caerulea*) which has a thick grey bill, blue breast and two chestnut wing bars. Indigo Bunting (*Passerina cyaena*), which is smaller, has a thick grey bill and a blue breast.
Status: Frequent resident (increasing in numbers due to concerted conservation initiatives).

Bluebird ♂

Bluebird ♀

Bluebird (newly fledged)

◆ 250. Hermit Thrush *Catharus guttatus*

Length: 6.5 inches (16 cm)

Identification: A shy and skulking thrush. Back, wings and tail ruddy brown. Conspicuous off-white eye ring and heavily speckled and streaked throat and breast, fading to flanks. Belly white, flanks suffused pale brown. Legs fleshy, beak black with base of lower mandible orange. Sexes alike.

Habitat: Mangroves, woodland, agricultural land, parks and gardens.

Similar species: Thrushes can be rather confusing to identify. Wood Thrush is *larger* with *bold black spotting continuing down belly to vent*. Veery has *faint grey* eye ring and throat speckling *fainter* and *less bold*. Both Gray-cheeked Thrush and Swainson's Thrush are *chocolate brown* on back, wings and tail and *lack* the rufous tint.

Status: Occasional vagrant.

◆ 251. Swainson's Thrush *Catharus ustulatus*

Length: 7 inches (18 cm)

Identification: A small thrush with chocolate brown head, back, tail and wings. Throat and breast buff and heavily spotted with brown. Buffy eye ring and cheeks. Pink legs. Sexes alike.
Habitat: Woodlands, mangroves and gardens.
Similar species: Gray-cheeked Thrush (*Catharus minimus*) *lacks* the buffy eye ring and has *grey* cheeks. Hermit Thrush (*Catharus guttatus*) *lacks* the buffy eye ring and cheeks and has a *red-brown* tail. Veery (*Catharus fuscescens*) is *paler*, *lacks* the buffy eye ring and has *faint* spotting on the breast. Wood Thrush (*Hylocichla mustelina*) is *more heavily* spotted with *black* and has *rufous* head, neck and back.
Status: Occasional migrant.

Family Mimidae (Mimic Thrushes)

(Total recorded: 2 species – Resident 1 sp., Vagrant 2 spp.)

◆ 261. Grey Catbird *Dumetella carolinensis*

Length: 9 inches (23 cm)

Identification: A slender, skulking grey bird with a distinctive cat-like call. Upperparts dark grey, underparts pale grey. Head has a black cap. Chestnut vent. Sexes alike.
Habitat: Woodlands, gardens, agricultural land and golf courses.
Similar species: Distinctive.
Status: Abundant resident.

Family Motacillidae (Pipits and Wagtails)

(Total recorded: 1 species – Vagrant 1 sp.)

◆ 264. American Pipit *Anthus rubescens*

Length: 6.5 inches (17 cm)

Identification: A small, slim pipit with a dark brown back. Wings brown, mottled with black, underparts buff and heavily streaked

Grey Catbird

with brown. Rump brown, tail black with white outer tail feathers.
Buff eye stripe and buff and black-edged malar stripe. Sexes alike.
Habitat: Agricultural land, fields, ponds, open areas and golf
courses.
Similar species: Northern Waterthrush (*Seiurus noveboracensis*) has
pink legs, *buffy* supercilium and *pale buff* underparts streaked with
black. Louisiana Waterthrush (*Seiurus motacilla*) has *pink* legs, *white*
supercilium, *white* throat and breast heavily streaked with *black*.
Status: Frequent vagrant.

Family Bombycillidae (Waxwings)

(Total recorded: 1 species – Vagrant 1 sp.)

◆ **265. Cedar Waxwing** *Bombycilla cedrorum*

Length: 7 inches (18 cm)

Identification: A delicately coloured and crested bird. Upperparts
chocolate brown with pale grey rump and a slate grey, yellow tipped

tail. Wings dark grey with red tipped secondaries. Throat dark grey, breast brown and belly buff. Black eye mask underscored with a thin white line. Crown and crest chocolate brown. Sexes alike. *Immatures* lack the red tip to the secondaries and have a more streaky appearance.

Habitat: Woodland, agricultural land, gardens and fields.
Similar species: Distinctive.
Status: Frequent vagrant.

Family Sturnidae (Starlings)

(Total recorded: 1 species – Introduced 1 sp.)

◆ 266. Starling   *Sturnus vulgaris*

Length: 8.5 inches (22 cm)

Identification: A medium-sized noisy, gregarious bird. Upperparts brown, underparts black with heavy white spotting and scalloping over entire body. *Breeding* birds become flushed with green and purple irridescence on head, back and belly. *Immatures* are a dull brown, ornamented with streaks of pale brown on the neck and breast.
Habitat: Urban, agricultural land, woodland, fields, cliffs, coast, mangroves, open land.
Similar species: Distinctive.
Status: Introduced, abundant resident; perhaps the most common species on the island, considered a pest species.

Family Vireonidae (Vireos)

(Total recorded: 7 species – Endemic 1 sub-sp., Vagrant 7 spp.)

◆ 267. Bermuda White-eyed Vireo   *Vireo griseus bermudiensis*

Length: 5 inches (13 cm)

Identification: A small, plump, inquisitive bird that can be readily identified by its distinctive 'Chick-of-the-village' call (which has given rise to its local name). Upperparts olive green, underparts pale grey.

Starling

Bermuda White-eyed Vireo

Lore and eye ring yellow, eyes white. Dark olive wing has two clear white wing bars. Flanks pale yellow and belly and vent white. Legs black. Sexes alike.

Habitat: Woodland, gardens and mangroves.

Similar species: Very difficult to discern from vagrant American White-eyed Vireos (*Vireo griseus griseus*), which is *brighter* in coloration and has *longer* wings. Solitary Vireo (*Vireo solitarius*) has *white* lores and eye ring and a *black* eye.

Status: Endemic sub-species, common resident.

◆ **271. Black-whiskered Vireo** *Vireo altiloquus*

Length: 5 inches (13 cm)

Identification: A medium-sized thin, skulking vireo. Upperparts dark olive, underparts off-white. Head has a pale grey crown, red eye, black eye stripe and a thin white eyebrow bordered above with

Black-whiskered Vireo

black. Distinctive black moustachial stripe (hence the term 'black-whiskered'). Legs black. Sexes alike.
Habitat: Woodland and gardens.
Similar species: Red-eyed Vireo (*Vireo olivaceus*) which is *larger* and *lacks* the black moustachial stripe. Warbling Vireo (*Vireo gilvus*) has a white eyebrow *without* a black border, a *black* eye and *lacks* the black eye stripe and moustachial stripe. Philadelphia Vireo (*Vireo philadelphicus*) *lacks* the black moustachial stripe, has a white eyebrow *without* the black border, a *black* eye and *pale yellow* underparts.
Status: Uncommon vagrant.

◆ **272. Red-eyed Vireo**   *Vireo olivaceus*

Length: 6 inches (15 cm)

Identification: A medium-sized, thin, skulking vireo. Upperparts dark olive, underparts off-white. Head has a pale grey crown, red eye, black eye stripe and a thin white eyebrow bordered above with black. Legs black. Sexes alike.
Habitat: Woodland, mangroves and gardens.
Similar species: Black-whiskered Vireo (*Vireo altiloquus*), which is *smaller*, has a distinctive *black* moustachial stripe hence the term 'black-whiskered'. Warbling Vireo (*Vireo gilvus*) has a white eyebrow *without* a black border, a *black* eye and *lacks* the black eye stripe. Philadelphia Vireo (*Vireo philadelphicus*) has a white eyebrow *without* the black border, a *black* eye and *pale yellow* underparts.
Status: Common vagrant.

Family Parulidae (Wood Warblers)

(Total recorded: 38 species – Migrant 8 spp., Vagrant 30 spp.)

◆ **275. Prothonotary Warbler**   *Protonotaria citrea*

Length: 5.5 inches (14 cm)

Identification: A medium-sized warbler often found in mixed-species flocks. *Males* have a bright yellow head and belly, olive back and white vent. Wings, rump and tail pale grey. Beak, eyes and legs black. *Females* similar to males but duller.

Habitat: Woodland, mangroves and gardens.
Similar species: Yellow Warbler (*Dendroica petechia*): males have a *yellow* back and vent, *grey* wings and distinctive *ruddy-brown streaks* on the breast; females have a *white* vent and *grey* wings. Blue-winged Warbler (*Vermivora pinus*) has a *black* eye stripe and two *white wing bars*.
Status: Frequent migrant.

◆ 281. Northern Parula   *Parula americana*

Length: 4.5 inches (11 cm)

Identification: A small, plump warbler found singly, in pairs or in mixed species flocks. *Males* have a blue-grey head, back and rump. Back has an olive patch in the middle. Throat and upper breast yellow, with a greyish brown band separating the two. Underparts white with some yellow and ruddy brown on the flanks. White eye ring split in two by a thin black eye stripe. Dark blue-grey wings have two white wing bars. *Females* similar to males but are duller and lack the breast band.
Habitat: Woodland, mangroves and gardens.
Similar species: Distinctive.
Status: Frequent migrant.

◆ 282. Black-and-White Warbler   *Mniotilta varia*

Length: 5 inches (13 cm)

Identification: A small black and white warbler found alone or in mixed flocks. *Males* have a body covered in alternating streaks of black and white. Distinct white supercilium, black throat, black streaked flanks and white belly and vent. *Females* similar to male but are duller and lack the black throat and black and white striped cheeks.
Habitat: Woodland, mangroves and gardens.
Similar species: Blackpoll Warbler (*Dendroica striata*): males have a *black* crown, *white* cheeks and a *brown* back streaked with black and white; females are *brown* with faint black striping. Yellow-rumped Warbler (*Dendroica coronata*): males have *black* cheeks and a *lemon yellow* nape, rump and side patch; females are *brown* and have a *lemon yellow* rump.
Status: Common vagrant.

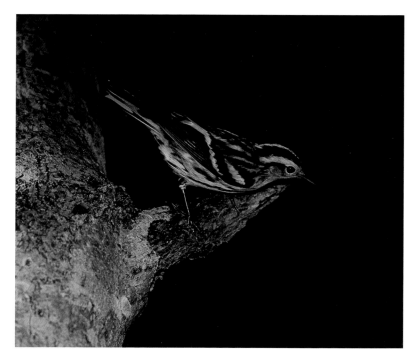

Black-and-White Warbler

◆ 283. Magnolia Warbler *Dendroica magnolia*

Length: 5 inches (13 cm)

Identification: A small warbler found singly, in pairs or in mixed species flocks. *Males* have a pale grey crown, dark grey back and wings and a black tail. Head black with thin white line above cheeks. Throat and rump lemon yellow. Underparts lemon yellow and heavily streaked with black. Conspicuous white wing patch and faint white markings on middle of outer tail feathers. *Females* similar to males, but slightly duller, with an olive back and two white wing bars on the wings.

Habitat: Woodland, mangroves and gardens.

Similar species: Yellow-rumped Warbler (*Dendroica coronata*); males have a *white* throat and underparts, a *yellow* patch on the crown and in front of the wing. Females are *brown-olive* with *white* underparts streaked with *light brown* and with a *pale yellow* patch in front of the wing.

Status: Occasional vagrant.

◆ **284. Cape May Warbler**   *Dendroica tigrina*

Length: 5 inches (13 cm)

Identification: A small warbler found singly, in pairs or in mixed species flocks. *Males* have an olive crown and back flecked with darker spots. Head dark yellow with a chestnut cheek patch. Underparts yellow streaked with black. Rump yellow, tail olive. Wings dark olive with conspicuous white wing patch. *Females* have an olive head and back flecked with darker spots. Pale yellow rump and yellow throat and belly streaked with black. Wings dark olive with conspicuous white wing patch.

Habitat: Woodland, mangroves and gardens.

Similar species: Although the male is distinctive, the female could be confused with the following species: (i) Pine Warbler (*Dendroica pinus*) has two *white wing bars* and *lacks* the black streaking on the underparts; (ii) Prairie Warbler (*Dendroica discolor*) has *black* eye stripe and malar stripe, *lacks* the black streaking on the breast and *lacks* the white wing patch.

Status: Frequent vagrant.

Cape May Warbler

◆ 285. Black-throated Blue Warbler
Dendroica caerulescens

Length: 5.5 inches (14 cm)

Identification: A very attractive warbler. *Males* have blue head, back, wings and tail, with pure white belly and white wing spot. The sides of the head, throat and sides are jet black. *Females* are olive brown on the head, wings, back and tail. There is a distinct buff eye stripe and a faint buffy wing spot. Throat, belly and vent buffy brown.

Habitat: Mangroves, woodland, parks and gardens.

Similar species: Males could be confused with male Cerulean Warbler which has *two white wing bars*, a *white* throat and *black streaking* on the sides. Females could be confused with Swainson's Warbler which *lacks* the wing spot, has *off-white* underparts and a *thick* eyebrow. Could also be confused with Palm Warblers, which have a *black eyestripe* and *two white wing bars*.

Status: Uncommon vagrant.

◆ 286. Yellow-rumped (Myrtle) Warbler
Dendroica coronata

Length: 5.5 inches (14 cm)

Identification: A medium-sized warbler often found in mixed-species flocks. *Males* have a pale grey head, back and wings and a dark grey tail, black cheek patch, white throat and lemon yellow crown patch. Underparts white with a large black chest patch and a lemon yellow patch in front of the wing. Wings pale grey with two white wing bars and rump lemon yellow. *Females* similar patterning, but brown instead of grey and black. Breast lacks black patch and is instead streaked with dark brown. *Non-breeding* birds are a dull brown, with pale yellow crown, rump and patch in front of the wing.

Habitat: Woodland, mangroves and gardens.

Similar species: Magnolia Warbler (*Dendroica magnolia*): males have a *lemon yellow* breast and throat, *lack* the yellow crown and patch in front of the wing and have a conspicuous *white wing patch*; females have *lemon yellow* underparts, heavily streaked with *black* and *lack* the yellow crown patch.

Status: Common migrant.

Yellow-rumped (Myrtle) Warbler

◆ **288. Black-throated Green Warbler**   *Dendroica virens*

Length: 5 inches (13 cm)

Identification: A small olive green warbler with a yellow face and olive ear patch. *Males* have a black throat, extending to black streaking on the sides. Wings black with two white wing bars. *Females* similar to males with yellow throat instead of black.
Habitat: Mangroves, woodland, parks and gardens.
Similar species: Adults could be confused with Townsend's Warbler, which has a *black* ear patch. Immature females are very similar to immature female Townsend's Warblers, but Townsend's has a more prominent yellow eye ring.
Status: Occasional vagrant.

◆ **294. Blackpoll Warbler**   *Dendroica striata*

Length: 5.5 inches (14 cm)

Identification: A medium-sized warbler often found in mixed-species flocks. *Males* have brown upperparts heavily streaked with black. Head black with large white cheek patch and black malar

Blackpoll Warbler

stripe. Underparts white with heavy black streaking on the flanks. Wings brown with two white wing bars. *Females* have brown upperparts streaked with black, buff underparts with faint streaking on the flanks. Wings brown with black streaking and two buff white wing bars. Head has buff supercilium. Legs pink. *Non-breeding* birds resemble females.

Habitat: Woodland, mangroves and gardens.

Similar species: Black-and-White Warbler (*Mniotilta varia*): males are boldly striped *black and white*, with a white supercilium and malar stripe; females have a *white* supercilium and are boldly striped *grey*, *black* and *white*. Bay-breasted Warbler (*Dendroica castanea*): nonbreeding birds very similar, but have *black* legs. Pine Warbler (*Dendroica pinus*): non-breeding birds very similar, but have *black* legs.

Status: Common migrant.

◆ **296. Yellow Warbler**   *Dendroica petechia*

Length: 5 inches (13 cm)

Identification: A small warbler found singly, in pairs or in mixed species flocks. *Males* have a yellow-olive head, back, wings, rump and tail. Underparts yellow and conspicuous ruddy brown streaks. *Females* similar to males, but lack the ruddy brown streaks.

Habitat: Woodland, mangroves and gardens.

Yellow Warbler ♂

Yellow Warbler ♀

Similar species: Prothonotary warblers (*Protonotaria citrea*) *lack* the ruddy brown breast streaks, have an *olive* back and *pale grey* wings and tail. Palm Warbler (*Dendroica palmarum*) has a *chestnut* cap and *brown* back, wings, rump and tail.
Status: Common migrant.

◆ **298. Palm Warbler**   *Dendroica palmarum*
Length: 5.5 inches (14 cm)

Identification: A medium-sized warbler often found in mixed-species flocks. *Breeding* birds have olive brown back, wings, rump and tail. Head has chestnut cap, yellow supercilium and black eye stripe. Underparts yellow and lightly streaked with chestnut. *Non-breeding* birds are similar in pattern, but duller brown, including the crown. Sexes alike.
Habitat: Golf courses, open areas, woodland, mangroves and gardens.
Similar species: Pine Warbler (*Dendroica pinus*) *lacks* the chestnut cap and streaks on the underparts and has two *white wing bars*.

Palm Warbler

Prairie Warbler (*Dendroica discolor*) *lacks* the chestnut cap and streaks on the underparts and has *black* streaks on the flanks, a *black* eye stripe and a *black* malar stripe.
Status: Common vagrant.

◆ 307. Ovenbird *Seiurus aurocapillus*

Length: 6 inches (15 cm)

Identification: A large, solitary, skulking warbler. Upperparts brown, underparts white and streaked with dark brown. Head has pale tan cap and white eye ring. Throat unstreaked and white. Legs pink. Sexes alike.
Habitat: Woodlands and gardens.
Similar species: Louisiana Waterthrush (*Seiurus motacilla*), which has a *white* supercilium, *thin* black eye stripe and *lacks* the white eye ring and tan cap. Northern Waterthrush (*Seiurus noveboracensis*), which has a *buffy* supercilium and underparts, *thin black* eye stripe and *lacks* the white eye ring and tan cap.
Status: Frequent migrant.

◆ 308. Northern Waterthrush *Seiurus noveboracensis*

Length: 6 inches (15 cm)

Identification: A large warbler that is often found on the edge of ponds, teetering back and forth like a Spotted Sandpiper. Upperparts brown, underparts buff with heavy brown streaking. Buffy supercilium and thin dark brown eye stripe. Legs pink. Sexes alike.
Habitat: Woodland, mangroves, pond edges and coast.
Similar species: Difficult to distinguish from Louisiana Waterthrush (*Seiurus motacilla*), which has a *white* supercilium, *unstreaked white* throat and *white* underparts.
Status: Common migrant

◆ 310. Common Yellowthroat *Geothlypis trichas*

Length: 5 inches (13 cm)

Identification: A small, generally solitary, inquisitive warbler. *Males* have olive brown upperparts and a yellow throat and breast. Face has distinctive black mask, bordered on the upper side by a thin white

Common Yellowthroat ♂

line. Belly off-white and flanks olive. Legs pink. *Females* similar to males, but lack the black face mask and have a very pale supercilium.
Habitat: Woodland, marshes, swamps and gardens.
Similar species: Kentucky Warbler (*Oporornis formosus*) has a *black* forehead, *thick yellow* eye stripe and *yellow* belly and flanks.
Status: Common Vagrant.

◆ 312. American Redstart   *Setophaga ruticilla*

Length: 5 inches (13 cm)

Identification: A small, inquisitive warbler that constantly fans its tail. *Males* are black, with red patches on the wings and on the middle of the outer tail feathers. *Females* have dull olive grey

American Redstart ♀

upperparts and white underparts. Yellow patches on the wings and on the middle of the outer tail feathers.
Habitat: Woodland, marshes, mangroves and gardens.
Similar species: Distinctive.
Status: Common migrant.

Family Emberezidae (Sparrows, Grosbeaks and Buntings)

(Total recorded: 23 species – Introduced 1 sp., Migrant 1 sp., Vagrant 21 spp.)

◆ 313. Northern Cardinal   *Cardinalis cardinalis*

Length: 8.5 inches (21 cm)

Identification: An unmistakable large, bright red bird with a prominent crest. Thick, cone-shaped red beak and black legs. Black face and bib. *Females* similar to males in pattern but are brown and buff overall, with reddish tint to tail, tip of crest and wings. *Immatures* similar to females, but are browner and have a dark bill.

Northern Cardinal ♂

Northern Cardinal ♀

Northern Cardinal (immature)

Habitat: Woodland, gardens, ponds, swamps, mangroves and marshes.
Similar species: Distinctive.
Status: Introduced, common resident.

◆ **315. Blue Grosbeak** *Guiraca caerulea*

Length: 6.5 inches (16 cm)

Identification: A small, chunky bird with a thick conical beak. *Males* are dark blue with blue-black wings and tail and a small black patch behind the beak. Wing has a thick chestnut wing bar and a thin tan wing bar. *Female* is pale brown with darker brown wings and tail. Wing has two tan wing bars.
Habitat: Agricultural land, fields, marshes and gardens.
Similar species: Indigo Bunting (*Passerina cyanea*): males are *smaller*, have a *smaller* beak, *lack* the wing bars and are more vibrant, *lighter blue* overall; females are *smaller*, have a *smaller* beak, *lack* the wing bars and have a *faint bluish wash* to the wings and tail.
Status: Frequent vagrant.

Indigo Bunting (mid-moult)

◆ 316. Indigo Bunting   *Passerina cyanea*

Length: 5.5 inches (14 cm)

Identification: A small, slender bird, usually found in small flocks. *Males* are bright blue, with blue-black wings and tail. *Females* have chocolate brown upperparts and buffy underparts. The wings and tail have a faint pale blue wash.

Habitat: Agricultural land, fields, marshes, mangroves, golf courses and gardens.

Similar species: Blue Grosbeak (*Guiraca caerulea*). Males are larger and darker blue overall. They have a thicker, larger beak and two wing bars (one thick and chestnut, the other thin and tan). Females are *larger* and *lack* the bluish wash to the wings and tail. They have a *thicker, larger* beak and *two tan wing bars*.

Status: Common migrant.

◆ 324. Chipping Sparrow   *Spizella passerina*

Length: 5.5 inches (14 cm)

Identification: A typical brown and grey sparrow. *Breeding adults* have a prominent white supercilium and a black eye stripe and black beak. Crown is chestnut and black, wings and tail are brown streaked with black. Nape, ear coverts and belly are pale grey and throat is white. There are two thin white wing bars. *Non-breeding adults* are similar in pattern to breeding adults but the supercilium is pale brown and the crown is buff, speckled with black. *Juveniles* are pale brown and grey and are heavily speckled with black.

Habitat: Agricultural land, mangroves, woodlands, parks and gardens.

Similar species: Clay-coloured Sparrow has *pale brown* ear coverts, belly *washed with buff* and *lacks* the wing bars. White-throated Sparrow has *black and white crown stripes* and a *prominent white throat*. The eyebrow shows *yellow* in front of the eye. White-crowned Sparrow has prominent *black and white* crown stripes and an *orange* bill.

Status: Occasional vagrant.

◆ **335. Snow Bunting** *Plectrophenax nivalis*

Length: 6.5 inches (16 cm)

Identification: A medium-sized plump bird often found in small flocks. *Breeding males* have a white head, wings, rump and underparts. Back and tail black. Outer tail feathers white. Tips of wings black. *Breeding females* have brown back and wings streaked with black. Head brown with tan supercilium. Wings white with black primaries and trailing edge. Tail black with white outer tail feathers.

Habitat: Fields and open areas.

Similar species: Distinctive.

Status: Uncommon vagrant.

Family Icteridae (Blackbirds and Orioles)

(Total recorded: 9 species – Migrant 1 sp., Vagrant 8 spp.)

◆ **336. Bobolink** *Dolichonyx oryzivorus*

Length: 7 inches (18 cm)

Identification: A medium-sized plump bird mainly found in large flocks. *Males* are black with a large tan nape patch. Rump and tail coverts white. Wings lightly streaked with tan and with conspicuous white shoulders. *Female* pale brown, mottled with darker

Bobolink

brown. Underparts tan and throat off-white. Brown eye stripe and a tan supercilium bordered on the top with dark brown.

Habitat: Fields, ponds and marshes.

Similar species: Male distinctive. Female could be confused with female Red-winged Blackbird (*Agelaius phoeniceus*), which has a *longer, more pointed* beak and is *heavily streaked* with dark brown.

Status: Common migrant.

◆ 344. Baltimore Oriole *Icterus galbula*

Length: 8.5 inches (21 cm)

Identification: A medium-sized, slender oriole found singly, in pairs and occasionally in small flocks. *Males* have black head, throat, upper back, wings and tail. Underparts, undertail, lower back and rump and outer tail feathers dark orange. Wings streaked with white and with a conspicuous white wing bar. *Females* have olive upperparts, dull yellow head, white throat, underparts and rump. Wings olive grey with two white wing bars. *Immatures* similar to females.

Habitat: Woodland, mangroves, gardens and golf courses.

Similar species: Orchard Oriole (*Icterus spurius*). Males *smaller* and have *dark chestnut* underparts and faint white streakings on the wings. Undertail *black*. Females *smaller* and have *olive yellow* underparts and *lack* the white throat.
Status: Frequent vagrant.

Family Ploceidae (Weaver Finches)

(Total recorded: 1 species – Introduced 1 sp.)

◆ 347. House Sparrow *Passer domesticus*
Length: 6 inches (15 cm)

Identification: A very common, familiar bird seen in noisy flocks. *Males* have brown back and wings mottled with darker brown and black. Wings have a single white wing bar. Crown pale grey with thick brown eye stripe that extends down neck to join at the nape. Pale grey and white cheeks. Black throat and 'bib'. *Females* have brown back and wings mottled with dark brown and black. Tan supercilium and darker brown cheeks. Belly tan and faintly streaked. *Immatures* similar to females.
Habitat: Cosmopolitan.
Similar species: Distinctive.
Status: Introduced, abundant resident, considered a pest species.

House Sparrow ♂

House Sparrows (immature)

Family Fringillidae (Finches)

(Total recorded: 9 species – Introduced 1 sp., Vagrant 8 spp.)

◆ **349. European Goldfinch** *Carduelis carduelis*

Length: 5 inches (13 cm)

Identification: A brightly coloured, diminutive finch, often found in small flocks. Upperparts brown, with black wings, white rump and black tail. Head black, white and bright red. Wings black with

European Goldfinches

large yellow patch and white edging. Underparts white, with pale brown flanks and breast. Sexes alike.
Habitat: Woodland gardens, fields and agricultural land.
Similar species: Distinctive.
Status: Introduced, frequent resident.

Family Estrildidae (Waxbills and allies)

(Total recorded: 2 species – Introduced 2 sp.)

◆ 357. Orange-cheeked Waxbill   *Estrilda melopoda*

Length: 5 inches (12 cm)

Identification: A medium-sized waxbill, found in flocks or pairs. Upperparts grey-brown, underparts pale grey. Head grey with conspicuous orange patches on side of face and orange bill. Throat pale grey. Red rump is a good identification feature. Sexes alike.
Habitat: Marshes.
Similar species: Common Waxbill (*Estrilda astrild*) has a *bright red* eye stripe, *lacks* orange cheeks and *lacks* the diagnostic red rump.
Status: Introduced, rare resident.

◆ 358. Common Waxbill   *Estrilda astrild*

Length: 5 inches (12 cm)

Identification: A medium-sized plump waxbill seen in small flocks. Upperparts grey-brown, underparts pale pinkish brown. Conspicuous bright red eye stripe and bright red bill. Throat white. Belly lightly barred, with a bright pink central patch. Sexes alike.
Habitat: Devonshire Marsh.
Similar species: Orange-cheeked Waxbill (*Estrilda melopoda*) which has a *bright red* rump, *orange* cheeks and *lacks* the bright red eye stripe.
Status: Introduced, rare resident.

Index

Note: page numbers in *italics* refer to illustrations separated from the text

cyanea 12, 113, 134,
135
Pelecanus
erythrorhynchos 14
occidentalis 3
Phaethon
aethereus 3, 49
lepturus 2, 3, 18,
19–20, 31, 32, 33,
34, 35, 48–9
Phaetusa simplex 7
Phalacrocorax
auritus 3, 49–50
carbo 3, 50
Phalaropus
fulicaria 6, 24, 84
lobatus 6, 84
tricolor 6, 84
Pheucticus ludovicianus 12
Philomachus pugnax 6
Phoenicopterus ruber 4
Picoides pubescens 9,
106, 107
Pinicola enucleator 13
Piranga
olivacea 13
rubra 13
Pitangus sulphuratus 9,
34, 107, 108
Plectrophenax nivalis 13,
136
Plegadis falcinellus 4, 58
Pluvialis
dominica 5, 71, 72
fulva 5
squatarola 5, 28, 71, 72
Podiceps
auritus 3
grisegena 3
nigricollis 3
Podilymbus podiceps 3, 46
Pooectes gramineus 12
Porphyrula martinica 5,
66, 67, 69
Porzana carolina 5, 66, 67
Progne subis 10, 111
Protonotaria citrea 11,
121–2, 129
Pterodroma
cahow 3, 18–19, 30–1,
47–8
hasitata 3, 48
Puffinus
gravis 3, 36, 47
griseus 3, 36
lherminieri 3, 36, 47, 48
puffinus 3, 36, 47

Quiscalus quiscula 13

Rallus
limicola 5

longirostrus 5
Recurvirostra americana 5
Regulus
calendula 10
satrapa 10
Rhynchops niger 7
Riparia riparia 10, 110,
111
Rissa tridactyla 7, 89

Sayornis
phoebe 9, 109
saya 9
Scolopax minor 6, 72
Seiurus
aurocapillus 12, 130
motacilla 12, 117, 130
noveboracensis 12, 23,
117, 130
Setophaga ruticilla 12,
131–2
Sialia
mexicana 45
sialis 10, 26, 45, 113,
114, 115
Sitta
canadensis 10
carolinensis 10
Sphyrapicus varius 9, 106,
107
Spiza americana 12
Spizella
pallida 12
passerina 12, 135–6
pusilla 12
Stelgidopteryx serripennis
10, 110
Steophaga ruticilla 2, 12,
131–2
Stercorarius
longicaudus 7, 85
parasiticus 7, 85
pomarinus 7, 85
Sterna
anaethetus 7, 91
antillarum 7, 92
caspia 7
dougallii 7, 90
forsteri 7, 90
fuscata 7, 91
hirundo 7, 20, 32, 33,
89–90
maxima 7
nilotica 7, 89
paradisaea 7, 90
sandvicensis 7
Strix varia 8, 103
Sturnella magna 13
Sturnus vulgaris 11, 24,
27, 35, 118, 119
Sula
dactylatra 3

leucogaster 3
Surnia ulula 8

Tachycineta bicolor 9,
110, 111
Toxostoma rufum 11
Tringa
flavipes 6, 75, 76, 77,
80
glareola 6, 75
melanoleuca 6, 76
nebularia 6, 76, 80
solitaria 6, 74, 75, 76,
80–1
Troglodytes
aedon 10
troglodytes 10
Tryngites subrufricollis 6,
28
Turdus migratorius 10
Tyrannus
dominicensis 9, 107
melancholicus 9, 109
savana 9
tyrannus 9, 107
verticalis 9, 109
Tyto alba 8, 33, 101, 102

Vanellus vanellus 5
Vermivora
celata 11
chrysoptera 11
peregrina 11
pinus 11, 122
ruficapilla 11
Vireo
altiloquus 11, 120–1
flavifrons 11
gilvus 11, 121
griseus bermudiensis
11, 26, 29–30, 31,
118, 119, 120
griseus griseus 11,
29–30, 120
olivaceus 11, 121
philadelphicus 11, 121
solitarius 11, 120

Wilsonia
canadensis 12
citrina 12
pusilla 12

Xanthocephalus xantho-
cephalus 13
Xema sabini 7

Zenaida macroura 8, 33,
98, 99
Zonotrichia
albicollis 13
leucophrys 12, 136